THE GLUE

WHY SALES & MARKETING MUST STICK TOGETHER

BY

GAVIN BELTON-ROSE

Copyright © 2025 Gavin Belton-Rose

All rights reserved.

No part of this publication may be reproduced, distributed, or transmitted in any form or by any means, including photocopying, recording, or other electronic or mechanical methods, without the prior written permission of the author, except in the case of brief quotations embodied in critical reviews and certain other non-commercial uses permitted by copyright law.

First published in the United Kingdom in 2025.

ISBN: 9798281247344

This book is a work of non-fiction based on the author's personal experience and professional practice. While every effort has been made to ensure accuracy, the advice and strategies contained herein may not be suitable for every situation or business. Readers are encouraged to consult with professional advisers before making any commercial decisions.

For more information, visit:

www.gainmomentum.co.uk

Cover design and layout by Gavin Belton-Rose

Printed and bound in the United Kingdom.

Contents

Who This Book Is For 1
Why I Wrote This Book 2
Author's Note 4

Part 1: Foundation & Philosophy 6
Chapter 1: My Journey 7
Chapter 2: Sales is the Engine 10
Chapter 3: Marketing Must Align 15
Chapter 4: The Real Role of the Business Owner 20

Part 2: Strategy & Structure 26
Chapter 5: Fixing the Disconnect 27
Chapter 6: Brands vs Leads 35
Chapter 7: Consistency Over Chaos 44
Chapter 8: Lead Flow & Conversion 52
Chapter 9: Time, Money & Focus 66
Chapter 10: Marketing Trends Are Not a Strategy 76

Part 3: Leadership & Leverage 87
Chapter 11: Your Strategy, Not Ours 88
Chapter 12: The Commercial Director Mindset 101
Chapter 13: How to Lead a Marketing Team 111
Chapter 14: The Invisible Drain on Your Sales 123
Chapter 15: Build It Around Your Life 133

PART 4: PRESENCE & POWER 141
   CHAPTER 16: VISIBILITY IS YOUR JOB 142
   CHAPTER 17: BE THE FACE OF THE BUSINESS 151
   CHAPTER 18: YOU CAN'T OUTSOURCE TRUST 160

PART 5: IMPACT & IMPLEMENTATION 169
   CHAPTER 19: THE GLUE IN ACTION 170
   CHAPTER 20: THE 6-MONTH GROWTH PLAN 179
   CHAPTER 21: THE GLUE IN PRACTICE: 20 QUICK WINS TO CREATE SALES & MARKETING ALIGNMENT 187
   CHAPTER 22: COMMON MISTAKES THAT KILL SALES & MARKETING ALIGNMENT 192
   CHAPTER 23: CHECKLIST SUMMARY: REAL-WORLD ALIGNMENT IN ACTION 199
   CHAPTER 24: ABOUT MOMENTUM – SALES & MARKETING, ALIGNED FOR GROWTH 205
   ACKNOWLEDGEMENTS 216

Who This Book Is For

This book is for people who want real growth—not just activity. It's for the business owner spinning all the plates, wondering why their lead generation isn't translating into revenue. It's for the sales leader frustrated with poor-quality leads and marketing that feels disconnected. It's for the marketer tired of creating content that never converts—because no one's following up. It's for the founder who wants to grow but doesn't want fluff, jargon, or theory that sounds great on paper and falls flat in the real world.

This is for the people doing it for real:

- The ones working with tight budgets, small teams, and high pressure
- The ones showing up to networking events, writing their own content, and doing their own follow-up
- The ones building something meaningful, not just trying to "go viral"

If you're tired of guessing, tired of hustle without results, and tired of being told you need more of everything—when what you really need is alignment—this book is for you.

And if you're ready to lead differently, grow intentionally, and finally make sales and marketing work as one?

Let's crack on.

Why I Wrote This Book

When I started out in business, I didn't have a playbook. I had instinct, hustle, and a deep belief that if I worked hard, I'd figure it out.

And I did figure it out—eventually. But it took years of doing things the hard way, building from scratch, rebuilding after burnout, and learning what no one teaches you: that sales and marketing are not separate. They are not departments. They are not opposing forces. They are the same conversation. And if they don't work together, your business doesn't grow—it just spins.

This book is for the business owner spinning all the plates. For the sales director frustrated with poor leads. For the marketer creating content that doesn't convert. For the founder tired of chasing tactics and trends that go nowhere.

I've worked across pubs, property, events, retail, sport, and service. I've started businesses, scaled them, sold them, and rebuilt after losing momentum. The one thing that's never failed me? Clear commercial alignment.

Not jargon. Not funnels. Not gimmicks. Just good strategy, executed well.

I wrote this book because I've lived this book.

You won't find fluff, recycled frameworks, or bloated case studies. What you will find is:

- How to think like a Commercial Director (even if you're a team of one)
- How to lead a team, align your marketing, and focus on what actually drives revenue

- How to build presence, trust, and momentum without burning out
- How to structure strategy, systems, and activity around the outcomes that matter

This isn't a corporate guide. It's a commercial one. And it's built for people doing it for real.

If you're ready to stop guessing, stop copying, and start leading with clarity—this book is for you.

Let's make sales and marketing stick together. Let's make it work. Let's make it grow.

Author's Note

My name's Gavin Belton-Rose, and I've been selling since I was 13. Not in a boardroom. Not in a training programme. In the real world. I started with two paper rounds. Then I stacked shelves at an off-licence. By 16, I was managing stock, watching salespeople, and unknowingly learning what would shape the next 25+ years of my life: how people think, how they buy, how they trust.

Since then, I've worked across sectors—hospitality, estate agency, events, marketing, retail, and sport. I've started businesses. I've scaled them. I've rebuilt after burnouts. I've worked with teams, led directors, closed deals, lost deals, won awards, and learned from every single one of them.

But if there's one lesson that's stuck with me, one truth that's shown up in every industry, every business, every challenge—it's this: **Sales and marketing cannot work in isolation. Not if you want to grow.** They're not separate departments. They're not rivals. They're not different teams with different targets. Sales is the engine. Marketing is the fuel. If they don't work together, you're not going anywhere.

This book isn't a theory piece. It's not full of fancy acronyms or complex frameworks. It's not here to impress the corporate crowd or get quoted in conference slides. It's here to help real people build real businesses.

It's direct. It's lived. It's what I know works.

You'll find mindset, method, structure, and strategy. You'll find stories that will sound like your own. You'll find lessons that have been tested and refined in the real world—not just made up in a marketing meeting.

You don't need more noise. You need clarity. You don't need to do more. You need to do the right things—together.

So whether you're running a small team, wearing all the hats, leading a department, or just trying to turn chaos into consistency—this book is for you. Let's make sales and marketing stick together. Let's make it work. Let's make it grow.

PART 1

Foundation & Philosophy

CHAPTER 1

My Journey

I've been selling since I was 13. Not in a fancy office. Not through online funnels. In the real world—on the streets, behind bars (the wooden kind), in people's homes, and face to face with customers. That's where the real learning happens. Not in a classroom, not on a Zoom call—but in the moments where someone decides to buy from you or walk away.

My first sales lessons came through two paper rounds and a job stacking shelves in an off-licence. That might not sound glamorous, but it was the beginning of everything. I watched how people made buying decisions. I listened to how regulars asked for what they wanted. I saw what products moved off the shelves and what gathered dust. I noticed what happened when you greeted someone with energy—and what happened when you didn't.

By 16, I wasn't just a shelf-stacker. I was helping with stock control, talking to suppliers, upselling to customers, and quietly absorbing how a business runs. That's something no textbook teaches you. I learned how to handle difficult people, how to stay calm when it's busy, and how to earn the trust of regulars. Every shift taught me more about sales than any course I've seen since.

Then came hospitality. The pub game. If you want to sharpen your commercial awareness, run a bar on a Friday night. It teaches you pace, pressure, and people skills. You learn to read body language, manage multiple conversations at once, and spot the moment someone's ready to buy. You learn to build rapport fast—and keep it. It's also where I saw what it takes to keep a team motivated when they're knackered, stressed, and working long hours. That's leadership, not just management.

Hospitality gave me thick skin. It gave me the ability to sell naturally, without scripts. It gave me stamina. That's something we don't talk about enough in business—how much stamina you need to show up consistently, stay focused, and lead from the front. Especially when you're the owner.

In my twenties, I moved through different roles—sales, management, business ownership. Every move added another layer to my understanding. I sold products. I sold services. I negotiated deals. I got told "no" a thousand times and still turned up the next day. I learned how to listen better. I learned when to push and when to pull back. I learned that selling isn't about pressure—it's about clarity, timing, and trust.

Eventually, I went all in. I became a business owner. That's when everything got real. I wasn't just selling someone else's product anymore—I was selling mine. I was responsible for marketing it, positioning it, pricing it, and delivering on it. That's a whole different level of pressure. But it also brought the biggest lessons.

I opened hospitality venues. I started a marketing agency. I launched a property business that became an award-winning estate agency. I experienced the excitement of growth—and the gut-punch of setbacks. I had team members let me down. I made hiring mistakes. I over invested in things that didn't return. But I also built something that mattered. Something people still talk about today.

Through it all, two things stayed central: sales and marketing. And I noticed something: they rarely worked well together in the businesses I encountered.

I'd see great marketers producing beautiful content, but no one following up the leads. I'd meet brilliant salespeople wasting time on unqualified enquiries because the marketing team didn't understand the audience. I saw budgets poured into brand awareness with no tracking, no calls to action, and no sales process to catch the momentum.

It drove me mad. Because I knew it could be different. I'd seen it work differently. When sales and marketing work together—really together—everything changes. Your lead quality improves. Your sales cycle shortens. Your conversion rate climbs. Your team morale lifts. You stop throwing spaghetti at the wall and start building something intentional.

That's why I started Momentum. To help businesses stop the madness. To stop the disconnect. To get their sales and marketing rowing in the same direction, with purpose.

Over the last decade, I've worked with companies across multiple industries—from retail and hospitality to tech, construction, sport, and service-based SMEs. I've acted as a fractional Commercial Director, guiding strategy, shaping campaigns, mentoring founders, and building systems that actually work in the real world. Not just PowerPoints. Not just pitches. Actual growth.

I've seen what works. I've seen what doesn't. And I've realised most business owners are not short on effort—they're short on clarity. They're doing too much. Or they're doing the right things in the wrong order. Or they've been told they need a fancy website, an ad budget, and a new funnel—when really, they just need a joined-up plan that starts with the customer and ends with a sale.

That's what this book is about. It's not theory. It's not fluff. It's not a repackaged sales course or a marketing funnel PDF. It's a lived, tested, stripped-back guide to what actually makes growth happen—when sales and marketing finally work together.

You'll find mindset. You'll find method. You'll find structure and strategy. You'll find examples from my own journey that will probably sound like your own. And you'll find a challenge—to lead differently, think commercially, and build something that sticks.

This is my journey. But it's also yours. Because if you've picked up this book, you already know something needs to change.

CHAPTER 2

Sales is the Engine

Let's start with a truth that some people don't want to hear:

Sales is the engine of your business.

It doesn't matter how great your brand looks. It doesn't matter how slick your social media presence is. If you're not selling—nothing else moves. Cash doesn't come in. Growth doesn't happen. People don't get paid. Sales is what drives it all.

For some reason, especially in the last decade, sales has been pushed aside in favour of marketing buzzwords, lead magnets, and online vanity metrics. We've got founders who obsess over followers, content reach, and impressions—but couldn't tell you what their sales pipeline looks like. We've got marketers creating beautiful campaigns that win awards but don't convert.

And then we wonder why businesses stall.

Let me be clear: I'm not against marketing. I run a marketing business. I believe in its power. But marketing without sales is like fuel without an engine. It might smell nice. It might get attention. But it doesn't take you anywhere.

Sales Comes First

In every business I've ever run, turned around, or helped grow, the first question I ask is: **where are the sales coming from?**

If that's unclear, everything else is noise.

You can't build a marketing strategy until you know:

- Who your ideal customer is
- What they need
- What you're offering them
- How you convert them
- What happens after the sale

Sales gives you the answers. Conversations give you data. Feedback from lost deals tells you more than any analytics dashboard. Sales isn't just about revenue—it's a listening post. It shows you what works, what confuses people, and what they're really willing to pay for.

The Sales-Led Mindset

Too many business owners hide from sales. They see it as scary, pushy, or beneath them. They outsource it too soon. They try to skip the uncomfortable parts. But if you want to grow, you have to face it head-on. You have to get close to it.

When I launched my estate agency, I didn't start by hiring marketers. I started by knocking on doors, making calls, introducing myself in the community. It wasn't about automation. It was about conversation. I learned what local sellers cared about. I heard their frustrations with other agents. I built trust.

That's what sales really is: **trust at speed**.

You don't have to be a natural-born seller. But you do need to lead with clarity, confidence, and consistency. You need to be visible. You need to be present. You need to be willing to ask for the sale—and handle it when people say no.

The Sales Process is the Business Process

Think of your business like a machine. Every part has a role—operations, delivery, finance, admin, marketing. But the engine? That's sales. And just like a car, if the engine's off, it doesn't matter how polished the paintwork is.

Here's a basic example I use with clients:

- **Lead comes in** – How quickly do you respond?
- **Conversation happens** – Are you qualifying them properly?
- **You offer value** – Is your messaging clear and compelling?
- **You follow up** – Do you have a system for this?
- **You close the deal** – Are you confident asking for the sale?

Most businesses drop the ball in one of those areas. And when that happens, no amount of SEO, paid ads, or viral content will save you.

Sales Reveals the Gaps

One of the reasons I love sales is because it's honest. Brutally honest. If something isn't working, it shows up in the numbers. If your team can't close, if your offer isn't strong, if your price point doesn't make sense—sales will tell you.

I once worked with a client who had thousands of social media followers, brilliant branding, and a slick website. But they were struggling to make consistent revenue. Why? Because they were generating the wrong leads. Their messaging was vague. Their follow-up was non-existent. Once we audited their sales process and made a few changes, things turned around in weeks. Not months—weeks.

That's the power of putting sales at the centre.

Sales Creates Momentum

The fastest way to build confidence in your business is to close a deal. Then another. Then another. Each sale creates momentum. It builds belief in your team. It generates cash to reinvest. It validates your offer. It shows you're doing something right.

When I launched Momentum, I didn't spend months perfecting a website or fine-tuning a logo. I got out there. I talked to people. I told them what I could help with. I listened. I followed up. I got results—and then I let the work do the talking.

That approach built the foundation of a business that now helps other companies grow. Not because we had a huge budget, but because we put sales first.

Sales Isn't Sleazy—It's Service

One of the biggest mindset shifts you can make is seeing sales as a service.

You're helping someone solve a problem. You're guiding them to a decision. You're making their life easier. That's not manipulation. That's value. The only time sales feels sleazy is when the product is bad or the intent is selfish.

If you believe in what you do, you owe it to people to sell it well.

When you avoid selling, you're not just hurting your business—you're withholding a solution from someone who needs it. Flip the script. Make it about them, not you. Ask better questions. Listen more than you talk. Follow through.

Your Sales Role as a Founder

If you're a founder, you are your company's number one salesperson. Even if you've got a team. Even if you hate the idea. You are the face, the voice, the decision-maker. No one sells with the same conviction as the person who built it.

This doesn't mean you have to be on the phone all day. But it does mean you need to:

- Be visible online and offline
- Be confident talking about what you do
- Set the tone for how your business sells

- Coach your team with real insight
- Understand your numbers and pipeline

Too many founders disappear into operations and leave sales to chance. Then they panic when cash flow dries up. Don't be that person. Build sales into your weekly rhythm. Make time for it. Celebrate it. Measure it.

Your Next Step

If you're reading this and thinking, "I've been putting sales off," now's the time to change that.

Go back to basics:

- Who do you help?
- What problem do you solve?
- How do you solve it?
- How can someone buy from you today?

Simple questions. Powerful answers.

Then look at your sales process:

- Are you responding fast enough?
- Are you qualifying properly?
- Are you following up?
- Are you asking for the sale?

Start there. Fix the leaks. Build your engine.

Because when sales runs well—everything else follows.

Marketing becomes more effective. Delivery becomes more predictable. Growth becomes more consistent.

Sales is not a department. It's a commitment.

It's the engine. And you need to start it.

CHAPTER 3

Marketing Must Align

Let's get something straight from the beginning: **marketing is not the saviour of your business if it's not aligned with sales.**

Too often, I walk into businesses where marketing operates like it's in a different building—sometimes it actually is. The marketing team is creating content, managing social media, sending email campaigns, even doing SEO—but when I ask how that connects to sales, I get blank stares. No one really knows what happens after the lead comes in.

Marketing without alignment is just noise. It might get attention. It might even generate a few leads. But if it's not leading people toward a sale—it's not working.

The Role of Marketing: Serve Sales, Don't Compete With It

Marketing isn't a vanity project. It's not about winning design awards or going viral. It's about **moving people closer to a buying decision.**

That means:

- Generating the right kind of attention
- Educating the audience
- Building trust and credibility
- Supporting the sales process

The purpose of marketing is to make selling easier. That's it.

Great marketing answers questions before they're asked. It filters out time wasters. It equips your sales team—or you, if you're selling—to show up with clarity, confidence, and context.

Marketing must speak the same language as sales. Same tone. Same urgency. Same focus on the customer's problems and outcomes.

The Disconnect is Real

Let me give you a real example. I worked with a business that had a brilliant in-house marketing team. Their content was polished, consistent, and full of value. But the sales team hated it. Why? Because it didn't support the conversations they were having.

While the sales team was talking to business owners about cutting costs and driving ROI, the marketing team was posting fluffy blogs about innovation and culture. It looked nice—but it didn't convert.

That's the disconnect. Sales and marketing working in parallel, not in partnership. And when that happens, both sides suffer:

- Sales blames marketing for poor leads.
- Marketing blames sales for not closing them.
- Leadership loses trust in both.

The real problem isn't either side—it's the **lack of alignment**.

Bridging the Gap

Here's how you bring marketing into alignment with sales:

Start With the Customer Forget about what you want to say. Focus on what your customer needs to hear. What are they struggling with? What are they trying to achieve? What are they afraid of?

Get Sales Involved in Marketing The best marketing ideas come from sales conversations. Have your marketing team sit in on calls. Listen to objections. Watch demos. Read email exchanges. That's where the gold is.

Set Shared Goals Marketing should be measured by impact, not just output. Likes, shares, and reach are nice—but do they lead to conversations? Are they creating pipeline? If not, what's the point?

Use the Same Language If your sales team is calling it "cost-saving tech," and your marketing team is calling it an "efficiency solution," you're creating friction. Agree on core messaging—and stick to it.

Create Content That Moves Every piece of marketing should move someone closer to a decision. That could be:

- Booking a call
- Downloading a useful resource
- Attending an event
- Requesting a demo

Awareness is fine, but action is better.

Content With a Commercial Purpose

This is one of the biggest shifts I help businesses make: getting marketing to operate with a commercial mindset.

That means every blog, every video, every post, every campaign has a job to do. It's not just content for content's sake—it's part of a system that moves the business forward.

- **Email marketing?** Not just pretty newsletters—strategic sequences that warm up prospects and get replies.
- **Social media?** Not just engagement—measurable clicks, DMs, and conversions.
- **Blogs?** Not just keywords—real answers to real questions your customers are Googling before they buy.

When marketing starts thinking commercially, everything changes. Your salespeople suddenly have assets they can use. Your leads improve. Your sales cycle shortens. Your entire business starts to feel more cohesive.

Marketing on a Budget Still Works—If It's Aligned

You don't need a massive marketing budget to see results. You need clarity and consistency.

Some of the most effective campaigns I've seen came from:

- A founder recording short videos answering FAQs
- A team member writing a weekly email summarising insights from sales calls
- A PDF guide built in Canva that addressed one specific pain point

Small actions, big impact—because they were aligned.

The problem most businesses face isn't a lack of ideas—it's a lack of focus. They're doing too much, trying too many channels, changing direction every month. That creates confusion internally and externally.

The solution? **Pick a lane. Align the message. Commit to it.**

Marketers: Ask Better Questions

If you're reading this as a marketer—either in-house or freelance—start asking better questions:

- What is the sales team struggling with?
- What objections come up most often?
- What language does the customer use to describe their problem?
- What's the next step after someone reads this piece of content?

Stop guessing. Get in the trenches. Be curious. The best marketers I know are basically part-time psychologists and full-time investigators.

Founders: Lead the Alignment

As the business owner or Commercial Director, this alignment starts with you. It's your job to:

- Set the tone for commercial thinking
- Break down silos between sales and marketing
- Encourage collaboration, not competition
- Hold both sides accountable to outcomes, not activity

If you let sales and marketing become separate camps, you'll waste time, energy, and money. But if you get them working together—you'll create something powerful.

Real Growth Comes From Integration

You don't need more content. You need more *connected* content. You don't need more leads.

You need *qualified* leads. You don't need more tools. You need a *strategy*.

When marketing aligns with sales:

- Prospects feel understood
- Sales conversations improve
- Conversions increase
- Customer experience improves

It's not about doing more. It's about doing it together.

Marketing must align. Because sales is the engine—but marketing is the fuel.

Let's make sure you're not pumping diesel into a petrol engine.

CHAPTER 4

The Real Role of the Business Owner

Let's be honest—most business owners are winging it. Not because they're lazy, but because they're wearing too many hats. One day they're head of sales, the next they're managing staff, the next they're sorting invoices and posting on LinkedIn. Sound familiar?

But here's the truth: if you're the founder, the business doesn't just need you to *do* the work. It needs you to *lead* it. And that means understanding your real role in the business—not just reacting to everything that comes your way.

You're Not Just the Boss—You're the Chief Energy Officer

People look to you. Your team, your customers, your network. They take cues from your energy, your confidence, your clarity. If you're tired, chaotic, distracted—that flows down. If you're focused, energised, and leading from the front? That's contagious too.

You don't need to have all the answers. But you do need to show up. Not just physically, but emotionally, commercially, and strategically. Especially in sales and marketing.

Visibility Isn't Optional

Too many owners want to hide behind the brand. They want the logo to speak for them. They want the content to do the heavy lifting. But people buy from people—especially in small to mid-sized businesses.

If you're not visible:

- You're missing trust-building opportunities

- You're relying too heavily on your team or freelancers
- You're creating a gap between your message and your market

You don't need to be a full-time content creator, but you do need to be present. At events. On video. In conversations. On your website. In your sales process.

You are the face of the business, whether you like it or not. So lean into it. When you do, you'll find:

- Sales becomes easier
- Referrals increase
- Brand recall improves
- Your team feels more connected to the mission

You Set the Standard for Sales & Marketing

Whatever you tolerate becomes the norm. If you're disorganised with your CRM, your team will be too. If you don't follow up, neither will they. If you treat marketing like an afterthought, guess what? So will everyone else.

As the owner, you don't need to do all the marketing—but you do need to drive the direction:

- What does success look like?
- Who are we speaking to?
- What's our tone?
- What are we trying to get people to *do*?

Same with sales. You might not take every call—but your team needs to see that you understand the process. That you care about conversion. That you track numbers. That you know how long it takes to close a deal.

You don't have to be perfect. But you do have to be present.

You Hold the Vision

It's your business. That means you carry the big picture. You know where you're going. You know what matters and what doesn't. But does your team?

Often, I'll meet owners who have all the clarity in their head—but none of it is shared with the people around them. That creates friction. Confusion. Wasted energy.

Your role is to communicate the vision. Constantly. Relentlessly. Until it sticks.

- Why do we exist?
- Who are we here to help?
- How do we do that differently?
- What does success look like?

When everyone knows the answers to those questions, everything aligns. Sales becomes more confident. Marketing becomes sharper.

Operations becomes smoother.

You Set the Culture

Culture isn't beanbags and free coffee. It's how people behave when you're not in the room. It's the standard. The rhythm. The way you show up.

Do you:

- Celebrate small wins?
- Call out sloppy behaviour?
- Share lessons from failure?
- Make time for development?
- Set clear expectations?

As the owner, you set the tempo. If you're late, distracted, or unclear—don't be surprised when your team mirrors that. But if you're focused, consistent, and committed to growth—they will be too.

Culture drives performance. And it starts with you.

You Lead the Commercial Rhythm

Let's get specific. Your role is to lead the commercial rhythm of the business. That means:

- Weekly check-ins on sales performance
- Monthly reviews of marketing impact
- Quarterly strategy resets
- Daily conversations that drive clarity

It doesn't need to be complicated. But it does need to be consistent. Your team should know:

- What we're aiming for
- Where we're at
- What's working
- What needs adjusting

If that rhythm is missing, things drift. Projects stall. People get busy—but not productive.

You Need Space to Think

Here's something no one tells you: your most valuable work doesn't happen at your desk. It happens when you give yourself space to think. That might be on a walk, at the gym, or with a blank sheet of paper.

Your job is to think strategically. That means:

- Spotting opportunities before others do

- Seeing patterns in the chaos
- Asking better questions
- Deciding what not to do

You can't do that if you're buried in admin. Delegate the noise. Create thinking time. That's not a luxury—it's your responsibility.

You Lead the Growth

At the end of the day, your role is to lead the growth of the business. That doesn't mean doing everything—but it does mean making sure everything is done well.

Growth doesn't happen by accident. It happens because someone is:

- Watching the numbers
- Protecting the margin
- Driving the pipeline
- Refining the offer
- Keeping the team focused

That someone is you.

If you don't do it, no one will.

Own It

You're not just a founder. You're not just the owner. You are the Chief Commercial Officer. The Head of Visibility. The Director of Momentum.

No one cares as much as you do. No one sees what you see. No one will drive it like you will.

Own that. Embrace it. Build around it.

Because when you fully step into your role, your team steps up. Your sales increase. Your marketing sharpens. Your growth accelerates.

And you stop being the bottleneck—and become the engine.

PART 2

Strategy & Structure

CHAPTER 5

Fixing the Disconnect

If there's one problem I see more than any other in the businesses I work with, it's this: sales and marketing are not on the same page. They might sit under the same roof, share some meetings, or nod in agreement on Zoom calls—but in practice, they're disconnected. And that disconnection is costing you.

It's not just a miscommunication issue. It's not just a clash of styles or targets. It's a full-blown commercial problem. One that creates friction, slows down growth, and leaves money on the table. Every. Single. Day.

This chapter is about fixing that. Not through fluffy team-building exercises or vague vision statements—but with grounded, practical strategies that actually work. Strategies I've applied across industries and companies. Strategies that turn isolated teams into a single, high-functioning commercial unit.

The Warning Signs: What Misalignment Looks Like

If you're wondering whether your business suffers from sales and marketing misalignment, here's a reality check. You probably do.

Some red flags:

- Marketing is chasing leads; sales is chasing revenue—neither is chasing results together.
- Salespeople think marketing is wasting budget on "brand" that doesn't convert.
- Marketers think sales aren't following up on leads properly.

- Content is being created, but no one uses it.
- Campaigns are launched with zero sales input.
- Sales decks and LinkedIn posts don't match the tone of your website.
- Leads are being handed over with no qualification or context.

If any of those feel familiar, you've got a gap. And that gap is costing you—through missed leads, longer sales cycles, higher churn, and inconsistent messaging.

This isn't just inefficient—it's dangerous.

Why It Happens (And Keeps Happening)

Let's break down the root causes:

1. Different Objectives - Sales is focused on revenue. Marketing is focused on reach. That creates conflict when marketing brings in traffic, but sales sees no conversion. Unless both teams are aligned to the same outcomes—measurable commercial results—they'll pull in different directions.

2. Different Timescales - Marketing tends to think long-term: campaigns, nurture sequences, SEO. Sales operates in the short term: targets, forecasts, deals to close this month. That gap creates pressure.

3. Lack of Feedback - Sales hears the objections. Marketing sees the engagement. But unless those insights are shared regularly and acted on, they never improve the shared strategy.

4. Siloed Systems - Marketing uses HubSpot. Sales lives in Salesforce. Notes never sync. Campaign data doesn't inform calls. And no one really knows what's working.

5. No Shared Definition of Success - One team wants more leads. The other wants better leads. But no one agrees what a good lead actually is. That's where the chaos begins.

6. Lack of Leadership Alignment - Often, there's no one owning the full commercial funnel. Marketing reports to one director. Sales to another. And both are fighting for resources without a joined-up strategy.

What It's Costing You

Let's be blunt. Misalignment is expensive:

- Your marketing spend is inefficient. You're generating traffic that doesn't convert.
- Your sales pipeline is clogged with cold leads.
- Your brand feels inconsistent across platforms.
- You miss out on referrals and advocacy because the customer journey is disjointed.
- Your teams become demoralised. People leave.

According to LinkedIn, companies with tightly aligned sales and marketing achieve 208% more marketing revenue and 36% higher customer retention.

If you don't fix the disconnect, your growth will plateau. No matter how much money you throw at ads or how many people you hire.

The Real Fix: Commercial Alignment

We don't want sales and marketing to "get along." We want them to operate as one system—a united commercial engine.

Here's how we make that happen.

1. One Commercial Goal

Scrap separate KPIs. Instead, define one primary goal that marketing and sales are both accountable for.

Examples:

- £500,000 in new revenue over 6 months.
- 100 SQLs per month that convert at 20%.
- 15 new high-ticket clients per quarter.

Make that the focus. Not impressions. Not click-through rates. Not meetings booked. Results. Commercial outcomes.

2. Joint Planning Sessions

At the start of every quarter, sales and marketing should meet to:

- Review the customer journey.
- Agree on campaign messaging.
- Identify gaps in content.
- Decide on follow-up strategy.

Don't leave it to chance. Book it. Run it. Make it part of your operating rhythm.

3. Define the Ideal Customer Profile (ICP)

Get everyone aligned on:

- Industry
- Role/title
- Business size
- Key pain points
- Buying signals

Once you know who you're selling to, everything becomes easier—from ad targeting to call scripts.

4. Qualify Leads Consistently

Define the following:

- What makes an MQL?

- When does an MQL become an SQL?
- What info must be captured before handover?

Use scorecards. Create qualification checklists. And automate alerts when someone reaches a score threshold.

5. Share the Funnel

There's no such thing as "marketing's funnel" and "sales's funnel." There's one funnel.

From awareness to advocacy—it's a single journey. Your job is to optimise every stage, together.

That means:

- Shared dashboards.
- Collaborative reporting.
- Reviewing drop-off points as one team.

6. Create Sales-Ready Content

Your marketing team should be feeding sales with high-converting content:

- Case studies
- Objection-busting one-pagers
- ROI calculators
- Video testimonials
- Competitor comparisons

Ask sales what content they wish they had—and create it.

7. Hold Weekly Debriefs

Every week, your commercial team should meet to review:

- What deals were won/lost—and why

- Which leads converted
- Which campaigns delivered
- What messaging landed best

This isn't a reporting session. It's a learning session. Capture insights. Action them.

8. Align Messaging Across All Touchpoints

Your website, ads, sales emails, and social posts should all tell the same story:

- Same pain points
- Same language
- Same promise

Consistency builds trust. Inconsistency creates confusion—and confused people don't buy.

9. Appoint a Commercial Leader

If you don't have someone responsible for overseeing the full revenue journey, you need one.

This could be:

- You (the founder)
- A Commercial Director
- A senior leader with both sales and marketing experience
- Their job is to:
- Set the strategy
- Keep teams aligned
- Report on shared metrics
- Hold everyone accountable

Real-World Example

One business I worked with had a £2,000/month marketing budget and a sales team of 3. But no shared process.

Marketing ran Facebook Ads, generating dozens of leads. Sales followed up manually. Results were inconsistent. Tension built. They blamed each other.

Here's what we changed:

- Aligned on the goal: 20 sales per month.
- Created a lead score system.
- Introduced a single follow-up sequence for every campaign.
- Set weekly reviews.
- Built a content library around common objections.
- Within 2 months:
- Conversion rates doubled.
- The sales cycle shortened by 30%.
- The teams started working together—not just side-by-side.

You don't need more money. You need better alignment.

Chapter Summary: Fix the Disconnect

- Misalignment between sales and marketing isn't a personnel issue—it's a leadership issue.
- The fix isn't a workshop—it's structure, rhythm, and strategy.
- You need one commercial goal, one funnel, one shared outcome.
- Run joint planning sessions. Share data. Debrief regularly.

- Equip sales with real tools. Get marketing into real conversations.
- Appoint a commercial lead to bring it all together.
- When you do this right, everything improves:
- Better leads
- Higher conversions
- Shorter sales cycles
- Stronger brand
- More predictable growth

Fixing the disconnect isn't optional. It's essential. Because until you do, your sales and marketing efforts will always be pulling in opposite directions—and your business will keep spinning in circles.

Now's the time to unify. To lead. To align.

This is where real momentum begins.

CHAPTER 6

Brands vs Leads

This chapter tackles one of the biggest false choices in modern marketing: brand-building versus lead generation. Ask ten business owners what they need more of, and five will say "brand awareness," while the other five will say "leads." Both are right—and both are missing the point.

You don't need brand *or* leads. You need brand *that drives* leads. You need visibility *that converts*. You need reputation *that results in revenue*.

The real goal is commercial brand-building—done in a way that drives measurable growth. This chapter is about aligning those two often-conflicted priorities and building a strategy that feeds both long-term equity and short-term cashflow.

The False Divide: Brand vs Leads

Let's be clear—this isn't a debate between art and science. This is about commercial impact. Somewhere along the way, brand and lead generation got siloed. One became the domain of agencies, creatives, and CMOs. The other, the playground of SDRs, funnels, and LinkedIn automation tools.

That's the problem.

In reality, the two are completely interlinked. A strong brand accelerates lead gen. And effective lead gen reinforces brand.

But many business owners fall into one of two traps:

Trap 1: Brand-Only Mindset

- They invest in logos, taglines, and clever campaigns.

- They prioritise awards and awareness over acquisition.
- They're well-liked in the market—but struggle to monetise it.

Trap 2: Leads-at-All-Costs

- They run aggressive campaigns with no regard for positioning.
- They burn out audiences with low-quality messaging.
- They hit short-term numbers but erode long-term trust.

Neither approach works on its own. The brand-first business stays broke. The lead-first business burns out.

You need a hybrid. A model where brand earns attention, trust, and credibility—while lead generation turns that equity into consistent revenue.

What Brand Really Means

Let's strip away the fluff. Your brand is not your logo. It's not your colour palette. It's not even your messaging.

Your brand is the *gut feeling* people have about your business.

It's:

- How you show up consistently
- The problems you solve
- The way you talk to your audience
- The trust you've built through your actions
- What people say about you when you're not in the room

And yes, it matters. Brand builds familiarity. Familiarity creates trust. And trust is what turns browsers into buyers.

But here's the key: that trust only matters if it *leads somewhere.*

A brand without a commercial mechanism behind it is just noise. But a brand with a strategic lead engine becomes unstoppable. When people trust you before you ever speak to them, you skip the hardest part of the sale: convincing them you're legit.

That brand gut feeling is shaped by everything:

- How your team answers the phone
- How quickly you follow up
- Whether your messaging is consistent
- If your values come through in your tone

It's holistic—and it's why brand cannot be outsourced entirely. It starts at the top.

Why Brand Without Leads Doesn't Work

You can be the most liked company in your space. You can post beautiful visuals. You can win awards. But if no one is entering your funnel or taking the next step—you're just popular, not profitable.

Brand equity without conversion is a vanity project.

You need to:

- Point attention somewhere
- Capture demand while it's hot
- Turn awareness into action

That means having clear next steps on your content. That means building marketing assets that are both on-brand and performance-driven. That means treating every piece of visibility as an opportunity to educate and invite.

Your brand should pull people in. Your lead strategy should show them the way forward.

The Brand-to-Lead Playbook

To connect brand and leads in a real-world, repeatable way, here's a five-step playbook you can implement in any business.

Step 1: Build Authority Through Consistency

Post consistently with your audience's pain points in mind. That doesn't mean churning out content daily—it means showing up on the platforms your audience uses, with value they actually care about. No fluff, no ego.

Use these pillars:

- **Problem-led posts** – Name their challenge clearly.
- **Proof posts** – Show results, not promises.
- **Process posts** – Share your method, show your thinking.
- **Personality posts** – Humanise your business and leadership.

Step 2: Create Demand Capture Points

Once you've earned attention, give people somewhere to go:

- Lead magnets with real value (not generic PDFs)
- Free audits, calls, or assessments
- "Start here" guides on your site
- Retargeting campaigns to keep warm prospects engaged

Step 3: Add Structured Nurture Sequences

Most leads don't convert right away. So don't lose them.

- Build 5–7 part email sequences that educate and invite
- Use objections as your content roadmap
- Mix automated and manual follow-ups

Your goal isn't to "sell"—it's to reinforce value, overcome fear, and keep the conversation alive.

Step 4: Activate Social Proof and Community

Turn existing customers into brand builders:

- Ask for testimonials at the point of highest satisfaction
- Use review snippets in your content
- Feature customer stories on LinkedIn or your website
- Build a community of advocates through simple referrals or branded groups

Word of mouth at scale starts with a brand people believe in—and a structure to collect and share those beliefs.

Step 5: Close Confidently

When your leads are pre-sold by the brand, the sales call is shorter, more focused, and less stressful. But only if your close matches your front-end brand.

Use a close script like:

"Sounds like we've covered your goals, clarified how we can help, and addressed the major concerns. Would it make sense to get this moving now?"

That soft, confident approach only works when the brand has already done the heavy lifting.

Example: From Cold Agency to In-Demand Partner

A small creative agency I worked with had relied for years on referrals. Business was okay—but unpredictable. They didn't have a lead gen system and were hesitant to "sell."

We repositioned the agency around a clear niche (property marketing), created a fortnightly LinkedIn post rhythm, and recorded short videos showing their design process. We launched a lead magnet: "7 Real Estate Design Mistakes That Cost You Sales."

Within 6 months:

- They had inbound messages weekly
- Their lead quality improved dramatically
- Prospects referenced specific content on sales calls
- They hired two more staff just to handle new work

They didn't become a "big" brand. But they became *the* brand in their space.

Common Mistakes That Break the Brand-Lead Link

Here are the red flags that signal you're getting this wrong:

- High ad spend, low conversion (leads aren't pre-sold)
- Website doesn't reflect your tone or value
- Inconsistent voice across social, email, and landing pages
- No follow-up systems for content downloads
- All content is "about you," not about the client

If these show up in your business, it's time to tighten the connection between what you stand for and how you sell.

Budget Allocation: The Balanced Model

You don't need to spend a fortune to make this work—but you do need a budget split that reflects where you are.

Here's a practical breakdown for small to mid-sized businesses:

Growth Stage	Brand-Building (%)	Lead Gen (%)
Early (0–2 yrs)	30%	70%
Scaling (3–5 yrs)	50%	50%
Established (5+ yrs)	60%	40%

Brand-building includes design, content creation, PR, video, and events. Lead gen includes ads, funnels, paid campaigns, and outbound tools.

This ratio should shift over time—as your brand earns more inbound attention, you'll need less push to generate demand.

Tactical Checklist: How to Align Brand with Lead Gen

Here's your 10-point action list:

1. Write your brand positioning statement (who you help, how, and why it matters).
2. Audit your website and social presence for consistency.
3. Create or update your lead magnet.
4. Launch a nurture sequence for new contacts.
5. Schedule two proof-based posts per week.
6. Interview one happy client and publish their story.
7. Add clear CTAs to every top-performing content asset.
8. Track branded search volume and direct traffic monthly.
9. Retarget engaged visitors with value-driven offers.
10. Review your brand-to-lead ratio every quarter.

Implementing this checklist monthly can tighten the commercial performance of your marketing and make every lead easier to close.

Additional Lessons: Where Most Businesses Get Stuck

It's worth looking at where businesses most often stall—not because of a lack of effort, but because of misalignment.

Case 1: The Silent Website

You've built a visually beautiful website. The branding is clean, the messaging is smart, but leads are non-existent. Why? Because there's no urgency. No clarity. No lead path. A commercial website isn't just a brochure—it's a conversion funnel in disguise.

Add bold CTAs. Break down your offer. Use video to humanise the process. Reinforce the visitor's pain, then offer relief. Your homepage should do the job of your top salesperson—quickly and clearly.

Case 2: The Ghost Campaign

You run paid ads that look good, sound clever, and deliver traffic—but no leads. That's because performance and brand messaging weren't synced. Your ads promised transformation. Your landing page offered features.

Always cross-check brand tone with lead generation intent. If your promise is emotional, your delivery must be too. If your CTA is commercial, your content needs to earn that ask.

Case 3: The Disconnected Team

Marketing is on one floor. Sales is on another. Neither speaks regularly. Marketing doesn't know what leads close. Sales doesn't know what messaging works.

Fix it with a monthly Commercial Meeting. One hour. Joint agenda. Data review. Objection sharing. Content requests. When teams align, results multiply.

Chapter Summary: Brand That Converts

- Brand and lead generation are not opposites—they're allies.

- Brand earns attention and trust. Leads capture and convert it.

- The strongest brands sell without selling—because they're positioned, consistent, and trusted.

- Avoid the trap of building a beautiful brand no one buys from—or running soulless campaigns that destroy trust.

- Use a clear playbook: Position → Visibility → Capture → Nurture → Close → Amplify

- Allocate budget based on your growth stage—and monitor ROI on both sides

When your brand works in sync with your lead gen, you stop relying on tactics—and start building momentum.

And momentum, not marketing tricks, is what builds a business that lasts.

CHAPTER 7

Consistency Over Chaos

When it comes to sales and marketing, most businesses don't fail because of bad ideas—they fail because they can't stay consistent.

One week they're active on LinkedIn. The next week they're rebuilding the website. Then they're at a trade show, then trying email again, then signing up for another CRM they'll never use.

It's chaos. And chaos doesn't convert.

This chapter is about rhythm. It's about doing fewer things, better. It's about building predictable, repeatable sales and marketing habits that outperform reactive campaigns every time. It's about making consistency your strategy—not just your goal.

Because in the real world, boring is what builds. The business that shows up every week with something valuable, with something real, will always beat the one chasing shiny distractions.

Why Consistency Matters More Than Creativity

Too many business owners confuse visibility with effectiveness. They chase likes instead of leads. They want to go viral instead of building value.

But here's the truth:

- Creativity gets attention. Consistency builds trust.
- Trust is what makes people buy.

Think of the businesses you follow or respect. It's not because they posted one great thing—it's because they showed up, again and again, delivering something useful, insightful, or honest.

Consistency compounds. It builds equity. It builds momentum. And over time, it becomes the engine that drives scalable, sustainable growth.

The Chaos Trap: Where Good Marketing Falls Apart

Here's what chaos looks like:

- No content plan or campaign structure
- Switching platforms or tools constantly
- New ideas every week, with no follow-through
- Relying on one-off events instead of systems
- Marketing that's reactive, not proactive

This is the business equivalent of sprinting in ten directions at once. You might be busy, but you're not going anywhere.

What starts as "being agile" quickly turns into inconsistency, missed opportunities, and wasted effort.

Worse still, this inconsistency erodes credibility. Your audience doesn't know when you'll show up or what you stand for. That uncertainty kills trust—and without trust, there are no conversions.

Repetition Builds Revenue

Great businesses don't change the message every month. They find a message that works—and then drive it home with relentless consistency.

Think of Apple. Nike. Innocent. They're not saying something new every time. They're repeating the same core values and promises in different formats.

In the small business world, you need to do the same:

- One clear value proposition
- Repeated across all channels
- With a consistent tone, style, and offer

The moment you get bored of your message is the moment your market is *just* beginning to hear it.

Framework: Building Your Sales & Marketing Rhythm

Here's a simple operating rhythm I've implemented with dozens of clients to replace chaos with consistency:

Weekly

- One educational LinkedIn post (positioning or value)
- One proof-based post (testimonial, result, or screenshot)
- Daily outreach (10–20 targeted messages or replies)
- Review active leads and follow-up steps

Monthly

- One blog or long-form content asset
- One newsletter or email send
- One content planning session (based on data + feedback)
- One team check-in on what's working and what isn't

Quarterly

- Full marketing and sales audit
- Campaign focus (one priority theme or offer)
- Review ICP and adjust based on actual buyer behaviour
- Clean up tools, systems, and messaging for alignment

- This rhythm isn't about doing more. It's about doing *enough*—on repeat.

Real-World Example: The Power of Boring

One of my clients, a local service provider, wanted to double their revenue. They didn't need fancy funnels or AI tools. They needed consistency.

We put a simple rhythm in place:

- Weekly post on LinkedIn (client wins, personal insights)
- Monthly newsletter
- Daily follow-up on warm leads
- Quarterly offer refresh with new case studies

Within 6 months:

- Inbound leads increased by 60%
- Close rate went up
- Website traffic became predictable

It wasn't flashy. It was boring. But it worked.

That's the point. Boring builds. Chaos confuses.

How to Spot When You're Slipping

Consistency is fragile. Even with the best of intentions, chaos creeps in. Here's how to spot the signs early:

- You start reacting to trends instead of strategy
- You miss one post… then a week… then a month
- You rewrite your messaging every time you get stuck
- You stop tracking what's working

- You delegate marketing with no direction
- If any of that sounds familiar, it's time to pause and reset your rhythm.

How to Stay Consistent (Even When You're Busy)

Let's be honest—business owners get pulled in a hundred directions. Consistency isn't easy.

Here's how to make it stick:

1. Choose Channels That Fit You

If you hate writing blogs but love talking, record videos or voice notes. Your system needs to work *for you* or it won't work at all.

2. Automate the Boring Stuff

Use scheduling tools. Use email templates. Set up reminders. Consistency thrives when admin is minimised.

3. Create a Bank of Reusable Content

Your best posts, emails, and scripts should live in a shared folder. Reuse. Reframe. Recycle.

4. Block Time Every Week

Make it sacred. Whether it's Friday mornings or Monday afternoons, build a routine. No marketing rhythm survives without protected time.

5. Build Accountability

Have someone who checks in on your progress. A VA, a partner, a mentor—someone who keeps the bar high.

Sector Snapshots: Consistency in Different Industries

SaaS: Consistency in User Education

SaaS businesses thrive when users understand the product—and that only happens through consistent onboarding, tutorials, and help content. The best ones:

- Publish weekly product tips on LinkedIn and YouTube
- Send monthly feature roundups
- Run automated nurture campaigns that guide users from signup to success

SaaS isn't won with a big launch. It's won with consistent post-signup support and visibility.

Local Services: Consistency in Presence

For local trades, coaches, or personal service providers, trust is everything. And trust is built when people see you *show up* regularly in the community:

- A monthly email newsletter to past customers
- A twice-weekly local Facebook/Instagram post
- Consistent Google review requests
- Quarterly flyers or community event presence

Repetition in a tight radius is what builds visibility. One-off promotions don't move the needle.

B2B Services: Consistency in Expertise

Consultants, agencies, and advisors win when they're seen as the expert. That means:

- A weekly insight post on LinkedIn
- Monthly webinars or email deep dives

- Repetition of key phrases, problems, and solutions
- Quarterly mini-campaigns aligned to seasonal client needs

This isn't about new content—it's about consistently delivering trusted thinking.

Campaign Layering: A More Advanced Consistency Model

Once the weekly rhythm becomes second nature, you can start layering campaigns across time.

Base Layer: Always-On Content

- Your weekly content rhythm (value, proof, personal)
- Organic presence (social, search, email)

Middle Layer: Monthly Campaigns

- One core theme (e.g. lead gen, trust, launch, event)
- Built around a specific CTA or offer
- Repurpose and repackage your message

Top Layer: Quarterly Growth Sprints

- A new strategic push: product launch, new segment, high-ticket sale
- Full alignment across sales, marketing, ops
- Content plan, nurture, email, and outbound

Consistency doesn't mean you're never creative. It means creativity has structure—and that structure builds momentum over time.

Chapter Summary: Predictable Beats Flashy

- Consistency builds trust. Chaos kills it.
- Most businesses don't need more ideas—they need more repetition.

- Repetition isn't laziness. It's leverage.
- Build your rhythm weekly, monthly, and quarterly.
- Use tools, routines, and accountability to keep momentum.
- Different sectors require different rhythms—but every business benefits from a consistent message, offer, and presence.

Consistency is not a "nice to have." It's the system that makes sales and marketing actually work—day after day, week after week, year after year.

Because in business, momentum belongs to the consistent.

CHAPTER 8

Lead Flow & Conversion

Most businesses don't have a sales problem. They have a flow problem.

They don't lack leads entirely—they lack the right flow of leads. They don't know where leads come from, what happens to them, or how many drop off without follow-up. They rely on luck, not a system.

This chapter is about building a real-world, scalable lead flow that converts. One that doesn't depend on you being in the room. One that works when you're busy. One that can be tracked, improved, and repeated.

You don't need a funnel full of names—you need a system that turns the right leads into real revenue.

The Difference Between Leads and Lead Flow

"Leads" are just names. "Lead flow" is a process.

It's the difference between someone filling in a form once—and a pipeline that fills, filters, follows up, and feeds your sales engine week in, week out.

Lead flow is how you:

- Attract the right prospects
- Qualify them based on fit and intent
- Move them through your system efficiently
- Convert them into paying customers

If you don't have clear stages, rules, and responsibilities—you don't have flow. You have friction.

Where Most Businesses Get It Wrong

Let's call out the common issues:

- **Leads come in from everywhere—but go nowhere.** No central process. No structure. They're scattered across inboxes, spreadsheets, or CRMs no one updates.

- **No clear lead stages.** Everyone defines "warm" differently. There's no standard for who gets a call, what counts as qualified, or when to follow up.

- **Follow-up is inconsistent or non-existent.** The biggest sales killer isn't a lack of leads—it's a lack of meaningful follow-up.

- **Marketing is judged by volume, not value.** MQLs, downloads, webinar attendees—none of it means anything if sales can't close.

- These problems aren't fixed with another tool. They're fixed with structure.

The Flow Framework: Awareness → Interest → Action → Conversion

Let's simplify lead flow into four clear stages:

1. **Awareness** – How people first encounter you
2. **Interest** – How you earn attention and qualify fit
3. **Action** – How they engage with a CTA
4. **Conversion** – The close or commercial step
5. Let's break it down.

1. Awareness: Start With Visibility

Lead flow begins with attention. But not just any attention—the right kind.

You need:

- Messaging that speaks directly to your ideal client's problems
- Regular visibility (LinkedIn, events, email, SEO, referrals)
- Clarity around who you're for—and who you're not

Awareness without targeting creates noise. Targeted awareness builds flow.

2. Interest: Hook and Qualify

Once someone notices you, the next step is engagement. But you need more than "likes"—you need signals of intent.

This might be:

- Clicking through to read more
- Watching a webinar or explainer video
- Booking a call
- Asking a question

Track this. Document it. Build your CRM to show where interest starts and what qualifies someone as ready to move.

3. Action: Move Them Forward

This is where a lot of businesses fall apart. Someone's interested—but the next step is vague or missing entirely.

Every channel must have a clear, low-friction CTA:

- Book a call
- Download a tool
- Start a free trial

- Join a waitlist

If people are showing interest but not taking action, you have a flow blockage.

4. Conversion: Make It Easy to Say Yes

Finally—conversion. But this doesn't just mean "buy." It means moving to the next *commercially meaningful* step:

- A paid discovery session
- A product purchase
- A proposal
- A signed agreement

Make this simple. Remove friction. Be clear about what happens next.

And remember: you don't close from scratch. You close from the context your lead flow has already built.

Qualification: Know Who's Worth Your Time

Not every lead is worth pursuing. That's why qualification matters. You need to build rules into your process that help your team (or you) spend time on the right opportunities.

Use a simple version of BANT or GPCT:

- **Budget** – Can they afford your service?
- **Authority** – Are you speaking to the decision-maker?
- **Need** – Do they clearly have the problem you solve?
- **Timeline** – Is there urgency to act? The goal isn't to disqualify harshly—it's to identify where to spend attention and how to follow up. You can tier leads into three buckets:
- **Hot** – They've shown clear need and urgency

- **Warm** – Interested, but may need nurturing
- **Cold** – Not a fit, or not now

Design automated workflows around this. Hot gets a call. Warm gets added to a nurture sequence. Cold gets retargeted passively.

Tracking: Make the Flow Visible

If you can't see your pipeline, you can't fix it. This doesn't need a £1,000/month CRM. You just need:

- Clear lead stages (New > Engaged > Qualified > Proposal > Won)
- A CRM (even a simple one like Trello, HubSpot Free, or Popcorn)
- A habit of updating it weekly

Your CRM should answer one simple question: "Who needs a nudge right now?"

Don't over-engineer it. A visible pipeline is better than a perfect one that's never used.

Follow-Up: The Revenue Multiplier

80% of leads don't convert on the first interaction. Follow-up is the single biggest missed revenue opportunity in small businesses.

Here's what solid follow-up looks like:

Day 1 – Thank them. Reconfirm the next step. Re-share your offer.

Day 3–5 – Add value. Send a case study, testimonial, or resource.

Day 7–10 – Ask a question. Invite engagement: "Has anything changed on your side?"

Day 14+ – Final call or offer to stay in touch. If no reply, move them to long-term nurture.

Use reminders. Use templates. But always personalise the first line. People respond to relevance, not robots.

Conversion Boosters: Close With Confidence

Once you've earned attention and trust, don't back away from the close. Make it frictionless and professional.

Here's what helps:

- Clear proposals with pricing, timelines, and deliverables
- Booking links (not email ping-pong)
- Option to ask questions or hop on a quick call
- A consistent sales deck that supports your pitch

And most importantly—confidence. If you believe in what you're offering, your leads will feel it.

Real-World Example: Local Lead Flow Done Right

One client—a home improvement specialist—was running local Facebook ads and getting clicks, but no sales.

Here's what we changed:

- Added a free guide: "Top 5 Mistakes Homeowners Make When Renovating"
- Sent automated follow-ups with case studies
- Pre-qualified leads using a 3-question form before a call
- Used a simple Trello board to manage each stage
- Within 90 days:
- Lead-to-call rate doubled
- Call-to-sale conversion went up by 42%
- Revenue became predictable

No complex funnel. Just structure, follow-up, and visibility.

Advanced Layer: Multi-Channel Flow in Action

For businesses ready to scale their lead flow, a multi-channel approach creates resilience and momentum. Don't just rely on one stream—build a blend.

Organic Inbound

- Weekly thought leadership posts on LinkedIn
- SEO-optimised blog content for specific pain points
- Strategic partnerships and referrals

Outbound Nurture

- LinkedIn connection + message flows
- Direct email outreach to a defined list
- Event or webinar follow-ups

Paid Traffic

- Retargeting to warm leads who've visited your site
- High-intent search ads for your top product or service
- Offer-specific landing pages with strong CTAs

Map these efforts onto your CRM. Tag the lead source. Track conversion rates by channel. Over time, this gives you real intelligence on what works—so you can double down.

Playbook Snapshot: 30 Days to Fix Lead Flow

Here's a simple plan any business can follow to improve lead flow immediately:

Week 1: Diagnose

- Map your current stages from first contact to close
- Review the last 10 leads: where they came from, what happened, what didn't

Week 2: Design

- Choose one lead source to focus on
- Write your lead stages on paper or whiteboard
- Define what qualifies someone to move forward

Week 3: Build

- Create follow-up templates
- Set up your CRM (or clean it up)
- Add one automated email sequence for new leads

Week 4: Execute

- Post value-led content 3 times this week
- Follow up on all leads in your system
- Review close rates, next steps, and gaps

Rinse and repeat. The more you review and refine, the smoother your flow becomes.

CRM Walkthrough: Set Up for Simplicity

A CRM shouldn't overwhelm you—it should enable clarity. Let's look at a basic but powerful setup anyone can implement:

CRM Columns (Kanban-style):

- **New Lead** – Entered from a form, referral, or manual input
- **Contacted** – Outreach has been made

- **Qualified** – Fit confirmed based on criteria
- **Proposal Sent** – Awaiting response
- **Closed – Won** or **Closed – Lost**

Key fields to track:

- Name, Company, Email, Phone
- Source (e.g., LinkedIn, Website, Event)
- Lead Score (1–10 or Hot/Warm/Cold)
- Next Step & Due Date
- Notes & History

Bonus Tip: Use automation to move leads between stages (e.g., Calendly integration moves someone from Contacted to Qualified automatically).

Templates That Make Follow-Up Easy

Initial Follow-Up (after download/contact):

"Hi [Name], just saw you checked out [resource/service]. If timing's right, happy to share how we've helped others in your space. Worth a quick chat?"

No Response Nudge (Day 5–7):

"Hey [Name], just checking in. No rush, but didn't want to drop the ball. Still curious about [problem you solve]?"

Final Check-In (Day 14+):

"Totally understand if now's not the time. Shall I circle back next month or leave it with you for now?"

These should live in your CRM or inbox templates and be used religiously.

Lead Flow by Sector

B2B Service:

- Weekly thought leadership post → Free checklist download → 5-email nurture → Discovery call

Consultancy:

- Event/webinar → Follow-up PDF → Book a 1:1 consult → Proposal

Retail/Consumer:

- Social content → Product page → Email discount → Abandoned cart follow-up

The structure doesn't need to be complicated—it needs to be followed.

Objection Handling by Flow Stage

Objections don't start at the close. They start earlier. Here's how to head them off:

Awareness – "I don't know who you are"

Fix: Increase consistency in content. Use recognisable hooks, tone, and visual branding.

Interest – "This might not be for me"

Fix: Use testimonials, case studies, and proof to match the message to the right audience.

Action – "I'm not ready to commit"

Fix: Offer low-barrier entry points. Discovery calls, free audits, helpful downloads.

Conversion – "I need to think about it"

Fix: Use urgency, simplify the offer, recap benefits and remove risk.

You don't need to become a sales shark—you just need to reduce friction and build trust at each step.

Lead Flow KPIs to Track

- **Lead Source Breakdown** – Where are leads coming from? Which channels convert?
- **Conversion by Stage** – How many leads move from New → Contacted → Proposal → Won?
- **Average Lead Time** – How long does it take to close?
- **Follow-Up Attempts** – Are you contacting leads 1x or 5x?
- **Revenue per Lead Source** – Which channel delivers not just leads, but value?
- Track these monthly. Use them to make better decisions—not just to report numbers.

Lead Handover: Sales & Marketing Alignment in Flow

Even with great lead generation and nurturing, if sales doesn't get a clear, contextual handover, leads fall through the cracks. Here's how to prevent that:

The Handover Checklist:

- Contact details with source tag
- Summary of lead journey so far
- Notes on objections, needs, timeline
- Next agreed action or booked call
- Any content they've engaged with

Whether you're solo or managing a team, creating this checklist saves time and shows your professionalism.

Tool Tip: Use shared notes in your CRM, or automate notifications to your sales inbox or Slack channel. That visibility shortens sales cycles.

Mistakes That Kill Lead Flow

Here are five of the most common mistakes I see that block lead conversion:

1. No defined process. If you don't know what happens to a lead from form to close, no one else will either.

2. Treating all leads the same. You need separate flows for cold, warm, and hot. Otherwise, you waste time or push too hard.

3. Not measuring time-to-response. If you wait 48 hours to reply to a form fill, they've already spoken to someone else. Speed matters.

4. Too much tech, not enough action. Buying CRMs, email tools, and dashboards doesn't make you consistent. Execution does.

5. No feedback loop. Sales needs to tell marketing what's working. Marketing needs to tell sales what leads are engaging. No loop = no improvement.

Avoid these, and you'll be ahead of most of your competitors.

Your Lead Flow Action Plan

This is the last section of the chapter—and where you put it all together. Here's a practical checklist to create or clean up your lead flow.

1. Map your funnel

- Awareness → Interest → Action → Conversion
- Label what assets or actions exist at each stage

2. Set qualification rules

- Define what makes a lead hot, warm, or cold
- Write a basic scoring system (or tiers)

3. Update your CRM

- Make your stages visible
- Ensure every lead has a source and next step

4. Create follow-up assets

- Write your email templates
- Record 2–3 value-based videos or audio messages

5. Align with your team

- Share your handover process
- Run a weekly pipeline review

6. Track the right metrics

- Leads by source
- Response time
- Conversion rate by stage
- Revenue by campaign

7. Review Monthly

- Block time to review your flow
- Kill what's not working, double down on what is

Implement this checklist, and your lead flow won't just improve—it'll become one of the most powerful systems in your business.

Summary: The Flow That Fuels Growth

- Leads aren't enough—you need lead *flow*
- A good lead flow system attracts, filters, follows up, and converts
- Use simple stages: Awareness > Interest > Action > Conversion
- Qualify quickly so you spend time on the right prospects
- Track your flow visibly—whatever tool you use
- Follow up like revenue depends on it (because it does)
- Make the close easy, clear, and confident
- If you want more sales, fix the flow.

Because a business with predictable lead flow isn't lucky—it's built that way.

CHAPTER 9

Time, Money & Focus

If there's one thing every business owner feels short of—it's time. And if there's one thing they're constantly juggling—it's money. But the real challenge? Focus.

You can find a bit more time. You can generate a bit more money. But if you don't know where to apply either—you waste both.

This chapter is about commercial prioritisation. It's not about working harder or longer. It's about knowing what matters most—and executing it relentlessly. Because not every task is equal. Not every opportunity is worth the effort. And not every sale is a smart one.

Most businesses don't fail because they didn't try hard enough. They fail because they misused their energy. They focused on the wrong channels. They over-invested in things that didn't move the needle. They outsourced core priorities and obsessed over tactics instead of strategy.

This chapter will help you stop doing that.

Why Time, Money & Focus Must Be Aligned

Let's get one thing clear:

Time is your only truly non-renewable asset. You can borrow money. You can earn more. But once time's spent—it's gone.

Money gives you leverage. It buys speed, talent, tools, and reach. But spent badly, it becomes a distraction. A vanity play. A sinkhole.

Focus is the multiplier. You can have all the time and money in the world, but if you're chasing the wrong metrics, talking to the wrong audience, or following someone else's blueprint—you're going nowhere.

Alignment means asking: Where do we spend time? Where do we spend money? And do those things directly support revenue, retention, or reputation?

Anything that doesn't—gets cut.

The Focus Filter: Commercial vs Operational Thinking

There are two types of activity in business:

- **Operational** – Keeps the lights on. Admin, accounts, fulfilment, internal communication.
- **Commercial** – Moves the business forward. Sales, marketing, customer relationships, reputation-building.

Most businesses spend 80% of their time being operational, and wonder why they aren't growing. The ratio needs flipping.

As a rule:

- If it generates revenue, gets leads, builds visibility, or creates referrals—it's commercial.
- If it keeps you busy but doesn't drive profit—it's operational.

You can't ignore operational work. But you must protect your commercial time.

Block it. Prioritise it. Defend it.

The Prioritisation Matrix: Focus on What Moves the Needle

When everything feels urgent, nothing gets done.

Here's a simple way to classify tasks and opportunities:

Urgency	Impact	Action
High	High	Do it first
High	Low	Delegate or drop
Low	High	Schedule it next
Low	Low	Cut completely

Apply this to your calendar, your to-do list, and your meetings.

Ask yourself: What are the 3–5 things this week that will actually move the business forward?

If it's not one of those, it's noise.

Budgeting Your Time for Commercial Return

You already know that your calendar is your strategy. So let's get tactical about how to structure your time for growth.

Break your working week into percentages based on commercial return:

- **50% Sales** – Calls, follow-ups, networking, proposals, referrals
- **30% Marketing** – Content, visibility, messaging, inbound campaigns
- **20% Leadership/Admin** – Team check-ins, reporting, systems

If you're in early stages or solo, you may need to go 70/20/10. The point is: over half your working time should be spent on activities that create cash or conversations.

Ask yourself weekly: What portion of my calendar created sales momentum?

If the answer is less than 50%, something's off.

Where to Spend Money (and Where Not To)

Here's how to think commercially about budget:

Invest in:

- **Lead Flow** – Ads, content, tools that attract and convert
- **Credibility Assets** – Case studies, testimonials, brand authority
- **Multipliers** – Software, contractors, or systems that save you time

Avoid overspending on:

- Overdesigned websites with no traffic
- Endless rebrands without strategy
- Courses and masterminds with no application plan

If it doesn't shorten the sales cycle, increase visibility, or remove workload—it's not a commercial investment.

The Toolkit: Routines and Resources That Protect Focus

Focus isn't just a mindset. It's a system. Here's what works:

- **Time Blocking** – Reserve hours for deep work, sales follow-up, and content creation. Don't leave them to chance.
- **Weekly Review** – What created revenue? What distracted you? Adjust accordingly.
- **Digital Boundaries** – Turn off notifications. Set email windows. Use Do Not Disturb like it's your job.
- **Simplified Tech Stack** – One CRM. One content tool. One email platform. Complexity kills focus.

Your goal is to make the commercial work *easier to start* and *harder to avoid*.

Think Like a Commercial Director

As a business owner, you wear many hats. But growth only happens when you step into your commercial leadership role.

Here's how to do it:

- **Zoom Out Weekly** – Review the numbers, pipeline, and lead sources.
- **Connect Sales and Marketing** – Treat them as a single system, not separate silos.
- **Push the Team to Focus on ROI** – Meetings, content, and campaigns should all pass the commercial test.
- **Remove Waste Relentlessly** – Kill weak campaigns, delete dead leads, and stop what isn't working.

Commercial directors don't chase busyness. They chase outcomes.

Sector Examples: Where Focus Wins (and Loses)

B2B Consultancy

- **Time waste:** Hours on proposal formatting, chasing poor-fit leads
- **Money sink:** Expensive branding without inbound traffic
- **Refocus:** Weekly LinkedIn content + 1:1 outreach = warm leads from real buyers

SaaS Founder

- **Time waste:** Endless feature tweaking instead of onboarding calls
- **Money sink:** Ads before product-market fit
- **Refocus:** Weekly demos and user feedback loops drove higher retention and word-of-mouth

Local Retail

- **Time waste:** Managing three social platforms with no engagement
- **Money sink:** Flyer drops without tracking
- **Refocus:** Email list + Google My Business reviews = sustained footfall and repeat visits

Focus wins when effort meets outcomes. Strip away the noise. Anchor your time and budget to what *works*.

How to Audit Time, Money & Focus (The 3-Column Method)

Take a blank sheet. Make three columns:

TIME	MONEY	FOCUS
Where do I spend hours?	Where do we invest cash?	What are we chasing?
Admin, delivery, reactive tasks?	Agencies, ads, tools, teams?	Engagement? Leads? Reputation?

Then ask:

- What creates results?
- What's unclear?
- What feels urgent but adds no value?
- Now score each item 1–3:
- 1 = Low impact
- 2 = Moderate
- 3 = High-value driver

Keep the 3s. Challenge the 2s. Cut or delegate the 1s.

Do this monthly. You'll become ruthless.

Distractions That Masquerade as Productivity

Not all effort is equal. Here are time sinks that feel productive—but stall growth:

- **Rewriting messaging weekly** – clarity comes from sticking, not switching
- **Over-reporting** – dashboards are only useful if they drive action
- **Meetings without agendas** – schedule fewer, shorter, and more purposeful sessions
- **Testing every new platform** – stay where your customers are

Productive businesses don't look busy. They look focused.

Decision Filters: 5 Questions to Stay on Track

Use these every time you're about to commit resources:

1. Does this support revenue, retention, or reputation?
2. Would we spend money/time on this again if starting from zero?
3. Will this matter in 90 days?
4. Is there a faster path to test or validate it?
5. Who owns this? And when will we review?

If you can't answer confidently—pause it.

Personal Focus Routines for Leaders

You are the pace-setter. If your focus drifts, so will your team's.

Daily:

- Morning review of top 3 priorities
- Protect first 2 hours for deep commercial work

Weekly:

- 1-hour performance review: leads, sales, traffic
- Calendar reflection: how much time went to ROI-generating activity?

Monthly:

- Kill something: a meeting, report, or task that adds no value

Focus is maintained by subtraction—not just willpower.

Overcoming Focus Fatigue: What to Do When You're Pulled in All Directions

Even with the best structure, routines, and tools, there will be weeks where everything feels like it's falling apart—client demands, staff issues, pipeline slowing down, personal commitments.

When focus starts slipping, here's how to recalibrate quickly:

1. Return to Core Goals What are the three outcomes that matter most this quarter? Anything that doesn't move those forward is background noise.

2. Use a Daily Anchor Commit to one non-negotiable focus action per day. A call, a proposal, a post—one thing that keeps the growth engine running.

3. Say No to More Things Busyness feels safe. Saying yes feels helpful. But growth requires ruthless prioritisation. Every yes is a no to something else. Practice it.

4. Write a 'Not-To-Do List' Document all the distractions you're tempted by: new tools, new services, vanity tasks. Keep it visible. Remind yourself that skipping them is a win.

5. Build Recovery Time You can't focus forever. Just like in sport, intensity requires recovery. Block 90-minute deep work sessions, followed by recovery activities—walks, resets, or light admin.

High performers aren't always ON. They're just intentional with when they are.

Strategic Delegation: Freeing Up Your Focus for What Only You Can Do

As the business grows, your most valuable work isn't doing everything—it's choosing what to *stop* doing.

Here's a simple rule:

Delegate anything that doesn't require your voice, vision, or relationships.

Use the Focus Delegation Grid:

Task Type	Delegate or Keep?	Why?
Invoicing	Delegate	Admin task with clear SOPs
LinkedIn engagement	Partial	Strategy is yours, execution can be supported
Proposal writing	Partial	Framework can be templated, tone is yours
Vision planning	Keep	Only you can do this

Start with 2–3 hours per week of focused delegation. Free that time for outbound sales, thought leadership, or customer feedback.

If you want to lead commercially, you can't be stuck in operations forever.

Summary: Clarity Creates Growth

- Time, money, and focus are your most valuable assets—but only when they're aligned.
- Commercial work should dominate your schedule.
- Budget must serve sales, visibility, or efficiency—not ego.
- Protect focus through structure, not just willpower.
- Lead your business like a commercial strategist—not a task manager.

You don't need more hours. You need more impact per hour.

And when every minute, pound, and decision is made with growth in mind—you'll get it.

CHAPTER 10

Marketing Trends Are Not a Strategy

In early 2023, I had a client come to me in a panic. They'd just seen one of their competitors post a viral video on TikTok, and within 24 hours, they were convinced they needed to shift their entire marketing strategy to short-form video content. The problem? Their clients weren't on TikTok. Their business relied on B2B referrals, long-term relationships, and industry trust. No amount of lip-syncing would help them close a £10k contract.

This isn't a rare story. Every week, business owners get distracted by trends that look powerful on the surface—but completely ignore the reality of their market, their offer, and their brand.

If you've been in business for more than five minutes, you've been told you need to jump on a new marketing trend. Maybe it was Instagram reels. Then it was chatbots. Now it's AI. And tomorrow? Who knows.

But here's the thing most people won't tell you: trends aren't a strategy. They're noise.

This chapter isn't anti-innovation. It's anti-distraction. Because for most business owners—especially those without big budgets or internal teams—chasing every new trend is the fastest way to waste your time, your money, and your energy. You're constantly reacting. You're always behind. And worse, you have no idea what's actually working.

Let's fix that.

The Problem With Trend-Led Marketing

The marketing world loves buzzwords. Every few months, there's a new "game-changer." But what actually changes?

Usually nothing.

Because trends don't fix fundamentals:

- They don't define your message
- They don't clarify your offer
- They don't build a system for leads and follow-up

What they do is distract. They create false urgency. They make you feel like you're falling behind—when in reality, you're just not doing the basics well.

Here's the truth: most small businesses don't need more channels. They need more consistency. They need a plan they can execute week in, week out, without constantly reinventing the wheel.

What Strategy Actually Means

Let's clear something up:

Strategy isn't about being clever. It's about being clear.

A proper marketing strategy answers five core questions:

1. Who are we talking to?
2. What problem do they have?
3. How do we solve it?
4. Why are we better/different?
5. Where can we earn their attention and trust?

Once you've got that, everything else becomes easier. Your content has purpose. Your outreach has direction. Your results are measurable.

Without it? You're just posting, hoping, and guessing.

Real Strategy In Action

Let's make this practical. Here's what strategy looks like in a small business:

Business: Local IT support company **Strategy:**

- Audience: Small businesses in the North West with 10–50 staff
- Problem: Slow systems and poor security
- Solution: Fixed-price managed service plans
- Message: "We make tech hassle-free for busy businesses"
- Channels: LinkedIn, referral partners, monthly newsletter

Everything they post, send, or say supports this plan. They're not dancing on TikTok or buying AI tools they don't need. They're focused.

Business: Family-run restaurant chain **Strategy:**

- Audience: Local families and professionals in a 15-mile radius
- Problem: Lack of consistency in dining options and experience
- Solution: Reliable, family-friendly dining with a loyalty programme
- Message: "Fresh food, fast service, local roots"
- Channels: Google My Business, local Facebook groups, monthly email list with offers
- No gimmicks—just a steady drumbeat of visibility and reputation-building.

Business: Independent career coach **Strategy:**

- Audience: Mid-career professionals in tech and finance
- Problem: Career stagnation and poor CV/personal brand

- Solution: 1:1 coaching with a focus on clarity, confidence, and visibility
- Message: "Unlock your next role with expert career support"
- Channels: Weekly LinkedIn content, quarterly webinars, free PDF guides

Each of these businesses uses strategy to cut through the noise.

And guess what? It works. Because strategy scales. Trends don't.

Let's make this practical. Here's what strategy looks like in a small business:

How Trends Should Be Used

This chapter isn't about ignoring trends. It's about using them properly.

Trends should be tested—but only when they support your strategy. Here's how to make that call:

Ask these five questions:

1. Does this trend help us reach our ideal client?
2. Can it amplify our message—not replace it?
3. Is it sustainable within our current resources?
4. Can we test it quickly without disrupting existing flow?
5. Will we know if it's working within 30–60 days?

If you can't answer yes to at least three—skip it. Come back later.

The Cost of Getting Distracted

Let's be blunt. Every hour you spend chasing irrelevant trends is an hour you're not:

- Following up on leads

- Improving your website
- Writing content that builds trust
- Reaching out to prospects
- Serving existing clients better

That's not marketing—that's noise dressed up as productivity.

It's also how businesses get stuck. They do "all the things" but nothing sticks. No growth. No momentum. Just fatigue.

Building a Trend-Proof Marketing System

Here's what I coach clients to build—a marketing system that works, regardless of what's trending:

1. **Core Message** Simple. Repeatable. Outcome-driven.
2. **Anchor Content** Weekly posts that solve problems, share wins, or teach something useful. No fluff.
3. **Follow-Up Process** Every download, enquiry, or lead gets a consistent next step.
4. **Primary Channel Focus** One or two platforms max. Usually LinkedIn and email for B2B.
5. **Monthly Campaigns** Rotate between offers, stories, proof points, and education.
6. **Quarterly Review** Audit what's working. Kill what's not. Adjust based on real data.

When that's in place, you can try trends—but you're not dependent on them.

Common Traps to Avoid

1. The "We Should Try…" Syndrome If it starts with "We should try…" and ends with no clear goal, bin it. Example: A team suggests a new podcast series but doesn't know who it's for or how it converts.

2. Vanity Metrics Obsession Likes don't pay bills. Neither do impressions. Focus on leads, meetings, and revenue. Example: A video gets 10k views—but no calls booked.

3. Complex Funnels With No Traffic Stop building five-step nurture journeys when you don't have 10 leads a week yet. Fix flow first. Example: You've got email automation in place but zero form submissions.

4. Tool Stacking Another software won't solve a clarity problem. Use what you have. Example: You sign up for three different CRMs and still forget to follow up leads.

5. Marketing Agency Dependence No agency can save a business with no direction. Own the message first. Then outsource. Example: You blame the agency for poor performance—but never gave them a clear brief.

What to Focus On Instead

Here's where your time and energy should go:

- Defining your audience's top 3 problems
- Creating simple, punchy messaging that speaks to those problems
- Writing helpful posts, videos, or emails every week
- Following up every single warm lead
- Asking for referrals and testimonials
- Reviewing your numbers monthly

Do that for 90 days and your pipeline will look completely different.

The Simplified Focus Map

Area	Weekly Action
Visibility	Post 2–3x about client results or common problems
Proof	Collect one new testimonial or screenshot a message from a happy client
Offers	Re-promote your core offer with clarity and urgency
Follow-Up	Call or message 5 old leads you've not closed yet
Outreach	Start 10 relevant conversations on LinkedIn

This is what real marketing looks like. It's not flashy. But it works.

Sector-Specific Strategy Over Trend-Hopping

Let's take a look at how this applies in different sectors, so you can see how to think strategically in your world—not just in theory.

1. Professional Services (e.g. Accountants, Solicitors, Consultants)

- Most common mistake: trying to go viral on LinkedIn with generic motivational quotes.

- Real strategy: Identify 3 common client pain points (e.g. tax deadlines, risk mitigation, compliance), and create monthly content plans around them. Host short, informative webinars. Write plain-English guides. Show authority through depth.

2. Trade Businesses (e.g. Electricians, Plumbers, Installers)

- Most common mistake: Using slick Instagram videos without showing pricing, process, or local availability.

- Real strategy: Focus on Google Reviews, FAQs on your site, and "Before and After" case studies. Add direct CTAs: "Call today for a free quote within 24 hours." Build trust with simplicity.

3. Hospitality and Retail

- Most common mistake: Dancing on TikTok without a brand or retention plan.

- Real strategy: Email newsletter for offers, loyalty programmes, Google My Business management, and customer-generated content. Make it easy for people to return, refer, and review.

4. Coaches and Consultants

- Most common mistake: Hiring someone to run ads before you've proven your message converts.

- Real strategy: Consistent video content on 1–2 platforms. A lead magnet that answers a real client question. Weekly follow-ups.

Testimonials and client story highlights.

Trends create spikes. Strategy creates a flow.

How to Build a 90-Day Strategy that Works

You don't need a 50-page strategy document. You need something you'll actually follow.

Use this structure:

Month 1: Foundation & Clarity

- Revisit your core offer. Who is it for? What problem does it solve?

- Create one-page marketing strategy: audience, message, main channel, primary CTA.

- Write 4 pieces of cornerstone content (1 per week) you can reuse and build from.

Month 2: Visibility & Consistency

- Post 3x per week. Use a mix of insights, offers, proof.
- Build your email list (offer a resource or checklist to download).
- Follow up all warm leads. Start a pipeline review habit.

Month 3: Feedback & Optimisation

- Ask: What got results? What didn't?
- Focus on top-performing content. Repurpose it.
- Automate 1 process (e.g. new enquiry follow-up email).
- Add 1 client testimonial to your website or proposal.

The goal isn't to go viral. The goal is to build momentum you can sustain.

What to Document in Your Marketing Playbook

This doesn't have to be fancy. Just keep it in a Google Doc or Notion page that you update monthly. Here's what to include:

1. Audience Clarity

- Industry, pain points, budget level, urgency triggers

2. Message & Value Proposition

- One clear sentence: "We help [who] achieve [outcome] using [method]."

3. Content Plan

- Weekly focus themes (problem, proof, value, offer)
- Calls to action (Book a call, Download, Join waitlist)

4. Campaign Calendar

- Seasonal tie-ins, product launches, content refreshes

5. Channel Strategy

- Where you're active (and where you've decided not to be)
- What you post and when

6. Follow-Up System

- How leads are tracked, who owns each stage, what reminders are in place

7. Results Review

- Monthly metrics: leads, calls, sales, top posts, click-through rates

When you treat your marketing like an asset, not an afterthought, it starts to work like one.

Final Thought: Play the Long Game

Key Takeaways from This Chapter:

- Marketing trends are tools—not direction. Don't confuse novelty for necessity.

- A solid marketing strategy starts with clarity: who you serve, what problem you solve, and how you communicate that.

- Trends can enhance, but never replace, a consistent message and clear offer.

- Focus on building a marketing engine that works with or without the latest trend.

- Time, money, and attention should be spent on assets that compound—content, relationships, and process.

- The goal isn't noise. The goal is predictable, sustainable growth.

Trends will come and go. Algorithms will change. New tools will appear. But if your business is built on solving real problems for real people, and you can communicate that clearly—then no trend will ever dictate your future.

Play the long game. Build trust. Focus on commercial outcomes. And remember: strategy isn't sexy, but it's what scales.

Show up. Say something useful. And do it again next week.

That's how you win.

PART 3

Leadership & Leverage

CHAPTER 11

Your Strategy, Not Ours

Here's the truth most marketers won't tell you: there is no one-size-fits-all strategy. What worked for a multimillion-pound agency won't work for a sole trader in Wrexham. What works for Nike doesn't translate to your local consultancy. And what drives leads for one business might completely flop for another, even in the same sector.

In this chapter, we step back from the theory, the templates, and the shiny methods. I'm not here to give you *my* strategy. I'm here to help you build *yours*.

Because real growth doesn't come from copying. It comes from clarity. From alignment. From decisions made with your market, your strengths, and your resources in mind—not from trying to bolt someone else's system onto your business.

If you're tired of the pitch-heavy playbooks and "7-figure frameworks," this chapter is for you. We're going to walk through how to build your own realistic, sustainable, and high-impact strategy—without relying on a guru, a gimmick, or a big marketing budget.

Why You Must Build Your Own Strategy

The moment you outsource your strategic thinking, you outsource your control. And here's what happens when people don't own their own strategy:

- They blame agencies when results aren't delivered.
- They bounce from idea to idea, never really sticking to anything.

- They struggle to explain what they do, who they serve, or why they're different.

- They constantly feel behind—always chasing, never leading.

Let me give you a real example. A local health and wellness company once came to me after spending thousands trying to replicate a digital agency's strategy they'd seen featured on a podcast. The agency served eCommerce clients. But the wellness company was trying to drive bookings for in-person sessions. They copied everything—the landing page style, ad copy, email flow. Six months later, they were burnt out, broke, and confused. Why? Because they followed someone else's roadmap that was never meant for their terrain.

A strong strategy gives you:

- Focus — You know what matters.

- Consistency — You do fewer things, better.

- Confidence — You know why something's working (or not).

We're not talking about a marketing plan you write and forget. We're talking about a living, breathing approach that anchors your actions and informs your decisions every single week.

You don't need a fancy document. You need clarity. You need conviction. And you need a system you'll actually use.

Strategy vs. Tactics: Know the Difference

Before we build, let's define. One of the biggest causes of confusion is people thinking tactics *are* strategy. They're not.

- **Strategy** is your plan — who you serve, what you offer, how you win.

- **Tactics** are the actions — what you post, where you show up, what tools you use.

If you chase tactics without strategy, you burn out. If you have strategy but never take action, you stall.

Let me give you a simple example. I worked with a small recruitment agency that was struggling with inbound leads. They decided to ramp up their presence on social media, posting daily on Instagram and Twitter—even though their target clients were HR managers in mid-sized companies, none of whom used those platforms professionally. They also spent time creating branded TikTok videos and email campaigns without a clear offer or sales flow. It looked like a flurry of activity, but it wasn't aligned to their strategy—because they didn't have one. The result? Burnout, no growth, and a complete re-evaluation three months later.

You need both. But strategy must come first.

A good strategy answers these five core questions:

1. Who do we serve?
2. What problem do we solve?
3. Why us — what's our angle?
4. Where do our people spend time?
5. How do we reach and convert them?

Once you've got this down, you'll never again feel the need to copy someone else's system.

The 5-Part Strategy Framework (That Works for Any Business)

Let's build it. Below is the exact framework I walk business owners through—no matter the industry, team size, or budget. Each part includes practical context and a common pitfall to help you apply it correctly.

1. Market Clarity Who are you for? Be brutally specific.

- Sector
- Size
- Pain points
- Decision-makers
- Buying triggers

If your answer is "anyone who…" — start again.

Example: A software company tried to sell to both schools and legal firms. The problem? Completely different needs, decision-makers, and buying cycles. Their message confused everyone—and they closed nothing. When they focused solely on schools and refined their pitch, sales tripled in six months.

2. Offer Definition What are you selling—and what outcome does it create?

- Is it a service or product?
- What's the transformation?
- What's your model (retainer, one-off, programme)?

Your offer must match your market's level of urgency, sophistication, and budget.

Pitfall: Too many small businesses bundle every service into one messy package. One client of mine offered design, print, digital, and video as one "marketing service." We separated it into clear, entry-level and premium offers—and conversions soared.

3. Positioning and Differentiation Why you?

- What are you known for?
- What do you *not* do?

- What beliefs do you stand by?

Positioning isn't about slogans—it's about perspective. What makes your approach distinct?

Example: A coach I worked with was struggling to stand out in a crowded space. Once they claimed their niche—helping neurodiverse professionals manage career transitions—they found their message and clients who valued that insight.

4. Channel Focus Where will you market?

- Pick 1–2 primary channels.
- Go deep, not wide.
- Match them to your audience's habits.

For B2B: LinkedIn, email, in-person events. For B2C: Instagram, local SEO, Google reviews, TikTok (maybe).

Pitfall: Don't try to be everywhere. One retail business I supported was posting across seven platforms with no real plan. We ditched five, doubled down on Google Reviews and Instagram, and finally got traction.

5. Sales Flow How do people go from stranger to client?

- Awareness
- Interest
- Decision
- Conversion
- Follow-up

If you don't have this mapped—even roughly—you don't have a strategy. You have scattered activity.

Example: A property firm used to rely solely on walk-ins and calls. We introduced a digital flow: free online guide → enquiry form →

phone consultation → valuation. Conversions improved by 40%, and their team finally had clarity on what leads were hot.

This framework doesn't require a big team or budget. It just requires attention and intent. Let's now take it into real-world examples so you can see it in motion.

Real-World Strategy Examples

Example 1: Solo Consultant — Leadership Development

- **Market:** Mid-sized companies with 50–200 staff in professional services
- **Offer:** 12-week leadership programme for new managers
- **Positioning:** "Real-world leadership training from someone who's built teams, not just studied them."
- **Channels:** LinkedIn and speaking at industry events
- **Sales Flow:** Free guide download → Discovery call → Programme enrolment

Example 2: Local Trades Business — Eco Heating Specialist

- **Market:** Homeowners aged 45+ in the North West
- **Offer:** Eco boiler installation with finance options
- **Positioning:** "Upgrade your heating, lower your bills, protect the planet."
- **Channels:** Google My Business, Facebook groups, door drops
- **Sales Flow:** Website enquiry → Home survey → Quote → Install → Review follow-up

Example 3: Niche eCommerce Brand — Golf Accessories

- **Market:** Men aged 30–55 who play regularly
- **Offer:** High-performance, stylish golf gloves and accessories

- **Positioning:** "Serious gear for serious players. Style and grip in one."
- **Channels:** Instagram, Facebook ads, influencer partnerships
- **Sales Flow:** Retargeted ads → Product page → Purchase → Loyalty follow-up

Example 4: Private Physiotherapy Practice — Healthcare Services

- **Market:** Active adults aged 35–65 recovering from injury or managing chronic pain
- **Offer:** 6-session rehab programme with personalised assessments and follow-up
- **Positioning:** "Move better, live stronger—expert physio built around your lifestyle."
- **Channels:** Google local search, local GP referrals, educational blog content
- **Sales Flow:** Initial enquiry → Free phone consult → Assessment booking → Treatment plan

These examples show that strategy isn't about doing more. It's about doing what works for you—and doing it consistently.

How to Validate Your Strategy

Once your strategy is built, you need to pressure test it. This is where most plans fall flat—they look good on paper, but don't survive contact with the real world.

Here's how to validate yours:

1. **Ask Your Market** – Run a few calls or quick polls with prospects or clients. "Does this message land? Is this a pain you're feeling?"

2. **Put Content Out** – Start posting based on your new strategy. Watch what gets engagement or leads. Don't expect viral. Look for resonance.

3. **Test One Offer** – Run a campaign for a single service or product. Use basic CTAs and measure interest, clicks, and calls.

4. **Use Feedback Loops** – Ask every prospect what they saw that brought them in. Use short surveys post-purchase.

It's not about perfect—it's about responsive. Strategy is a working document, not a monument.

Don't Copy—Adapt

Here's a reality check. The top businesses you admire? They didn't copy. They adapted. They took principles and tailored them. They learned from what worked elsewhere, but built what worked *here*.

If your business is in early growth, your strategy will look different to a 10-year-old brand. If you're selling to large corporates, you won't rely on daily Instagram posts. If you're a solopreneur, you'll need more automation and less complexity.

Use examples for inspiration. But always run them through your own filter:

- Do I have the resources to do this?
- Does this speak to *my* customer?
- Does this reflect how I want to show up?

If not—don't do it.

Strategic Patience: Give It Time

One of the biggest killers of momentum is impatience.

You build a strategy. You start executing. But within two weeks, you feel like it's not working—so you tweak it. Or switch gears. Or chase a trend.

Give your system 60–90 days of focused, consistent effort before making big changes. Small refinements are fine—but don't rebuild the engine every time the car hits a speed bump.

Consistency wins. Not because it's flashy, but because it compounds.

If you post once a week for a year, that's 52 data points. 52 touchpoints. 52 chances to build trust. Compare that to one "campaign" every few months that never gets traction.

Don't be seduced by the fast fix. Be committed to the right next step.

Your Strategic Checklist

Before we close this chapter, here's a practical checklist to help you lock in your own strategy.

Clarity

- I know who I serve (with specific details)
- I know the top 3 problems I solve
- I've got one main offer or product to promote

Positioning

- I can explain what makes us different in one sentence
- I'm clear about what we *don't* do

Channel Focus

- I've chosen 1–2 channels to go deep on
- I know what content belongs where

Sales Flow

- I have mapped how leads find, engage, and buy from me
- There's a clear follow-up process in place

Execution

- I can stick to this plan for 90 days
- I've got tools or people in place to help deliver

If you tick most of these—you're ready to grow. If not, that's your next task.

Strategic Mistakes That Kill Momentum

Before we close out this chapter, let's address the most common strategic errors that quietly sabotage growth. These are the pitfalls I see again and again when working with business owners who *think* they have a strategy—but don't.

1. Mistaking Activity for Progress Just because you're busy doesn't mean you're building. Marketing without strategy leads to motion, not momentum. Endless content, meetings, outreach—but no clear destination.

2. Pivoting Too Soon It's easy to panic when leads are slow. But changing your strategy every 30 days means nothing compounds. Stick to the plan, measure the right things, and refine based on data—not emotions.

3. Abdicating Ownership to a Third Party This is one of the most damaging mistakes I see. Business owners hand off their marketing or sales entirely to an agency, freelancer, or junior team member without leading the strategy themselves. Then they're shocked when results don't follow. Agencies can support delivery—but they can't define your voice, your value, or your position. That's your job.

4. Thinking Strategy Is Just for Big Companies It's not. In fact, smaller teams need strategy *more*. You don't have the luxury of wasted time, money, or staff. Your focus has to be tighter. Your systems cleaner. Your alignment sharper.

5. Overcomplicating Everything If your marketing strategy can't fit on one page or be explained in under two minutes, it's probably too complex. That means no one follows it. Keep it tight. Keep it real. Keep it relevant.

Tools to Simplify Strategy Execution

It's one thing to have a strategy. It's another to actually use it.

Here are the tools I recommend to keep your strategy visible, usable, and actionable:

1. The One-Pager Strategy Map Use a single Google Doc or Notion page with the five core areas:

- Audience
- Offer
- Positioning
- Channels
- Sales Flow

Update monthly. Share with your team. Print it out and stick it to your wall.

2. Weekly Scorecard Track the *inputs* that feed your results:

- How many content pieces published?
- How many new leads?
- How many follow-ups?
- How many calls booked?

Inputs drive outputs. Get religious about this.

3. Campaign Calendar Use a spreadsheet or whiteboard to plan your next 4–6 weeks of marketing. Don't wing it. Schedule the rhythm:

- Week 1: Proof content + offer push
- Week 2: Education piece + story
- Week 3: Client spotlight + lead magnet
- Week 4: Direct CTA + case study

You can repeat this forever—just rotate the assets.

4. CRM or Simple Pipeline Board Use Popcorn, Trello, HubSpot Free—whatever works for your brain. But make sure:

- You track where leads are in the journey
- You know who needs a follow-up
- You can see how long people have been sitting in a stage

If it's not visible, it doesn't exist.

Strategy Is a Skill — Learn It, Don't Lease It

Here's the mindset shift I want to leave you with:

Your ability to think strategically is a competitive advantage. Learn it like a skill.

Strategy is not a mystical art. It's not something reserved for Harvard MBAs or corporate marketing departments. It's a discipline. One that gets sharper with practice.

Every time you:

- Clarify your audience
- Tighten your message
- Simplify your offer
- Refine your process
- Measure what matters

You're building strategic muscle. And just like in the gym, consistency is everything.

Strategy is what makes you resilient when the algorithm changes. When your ads stop working. When your biggest referral source dries up. Strategy gives you alternatives. It gives you context. It gives you control.

Stop looking for a hero strategy to save you. Build your own.

Summary: Your Strategy, Your Success

- Strategy isn't about complexity—it's about clarity.
- Don't borrow someone else's blueprint. Build your own.
- Anchor your actions in who you help and how you solve their problems.
- Pick the right channels. Stick to them.
- Validate, review, refine—but don't flinch every time things are slow.

You don't need more noise. You need alignment. And that only comes when you commit to your own approach.

Your strategy should sound like you, feel like you, and work for you.

No gimmicks. No guessing. Just growth—on your terms.

That's your next chapter.

CHAPTER 12

The Commercial Director Mindset

When most people hear the word "director," they think of someone sitting in a glass office, far removed from the day-to-day. But a true Commercial Director? They're in the trenches—thinking strategically, leading cross-functional efforts, and constantly hunting for ways to drive revenue without burning bridges or budgets.

This chapter isn't about giving yourself a new title. It's about adopting the mindset of someone who leads the commercial heartbeat of a business. Whether you're a solo founder, a growing SME owner, or managing a small team—developing this way of thinking will shift the way you make decisions, run your sales and marketing, and measure success.

Because what your business really needs isn't more content or another sales tool. It needs someone steering the ship with clarity, confidence, and commercial sense. Let's make that person you.

What Is the Commercial Director Mindset?

The Commercial Director Mindset is about owning responsibility for all things growth—revenue, relationships, retention, and reputation. It's the glue between sales, marketing, operations, and customer experience. It's not about micromanaging every task—it's about overseeing outcomes and ensuring everything contributes to the commercial success of the business.

A true Commercial Director doesn't just ask "What should we do?" They ask:

- "What are we trying to achieve commercially?"

- "What's the opportunity cost?"
- "Where are we leaking revenue?"
- "What's the next best step for sustainable growth?"

This mindset is rare in small businesses—not because people aren't capable, but because they're stuck in reactive mode. When you're wearing all the hats, it's easy to default to doing rather than directing.

But the shift is necessary if you want to move from busyness to business growth. Operating from this mindset helps you zoom out, make strategic decisions based on real numbers, and course-correct before small problems become crises.

Contrast Example: Imagine two small business owners. One wakes up and checks emails, responding to every client message, posting on social media, and spinning plates all day. The other starts the day reviewing pipeline movement, identifying bottlenecks, assigning action, and prioritising two key revenue-generating activities. Guess which one finishes the week with measurable progress?

This mindset is not about doing more—it's about doing what matters.

Five Pillars of the Commercial Director Mindset

Let's break it down into five core behaviours that shape this way of thinking:

1. Lead With Revenue in Mind

Everything starts here. A Commercial Director doesn't view marketing as fluff or brand as vanity. They ask: "How does this drive income, now or later?"

That doesn't mean you focus only on fast sales. It means everything needs a role in the revenue story—whether it's short-term lead gen, long-term brand building, or improving retention.

Real-world mistake: I worked with a founder who was running high-engagement email campaigns filled with insights and tips. People loved the emails—but there was no call to action, no offer, no progression. When we added a simple CTA at the end of every email—booking a free 15-minute consult—leads increased by 230% in four weeks. Same emails, just commercially aligned.

A Commercial Director knows that great marketing isn't just expressive—it's effective.

2. Connect Departments, Don't Separate Them

Revenue lives in the gaps. When marketing doesn't speak to sales, or sales doesn't inform delivery, opportunities fall through the cracks.

You must become the bridge.

Commercial thinkers create feedback loops. They bring marketers into sales debriefs. They show delivery teams the lifetime value of a well-handled customer. They unify the business under one outcome: growth with integrity.

Action tip: Start by holding a simple monthly commercial alignment session with all key players—even if that's just you and two others. Review:

- Lead quality
- Client feedback
- Sales cycle performance
- Messaging accuracy
- Delivery challenges

Alignment isn't a buzzword. It's a business advantage.

3. Think in Systems, Not Surges

Too many small businesses rely on reactive marketing. They wait until leads dry up, then panic-post or discount. Then they're flooded, overwhelmed, drop the ball—and repeat the cycle.

A Commercial Director breaks that cycle by building systems:

- Evergreen nurture sequences
- CRM-based pipeline tracking
- Weekly follow-up tasks
- Monthly campaign planning

They understand that a good month should be repeatable—not a fluke. They view every win as something to document and improve.

Framework: Build one system per quarter. Don't try to overhaul everything at once. Start with lead capture and follow-up. Then move to onboarding. Then referrals. Layer success.

4. Prioritise Return, Not Busyness

Being busy doesn't mean you're being effective. The Commercial Director mindset forces you to constantly ask:

- "Is this driving a measurable result?"
- "Can someone else do this better or cheaper?"
- "Does this task align with our top priorities?"

It also means ruthless time protection. Commercial thinkers schedule sales time, review time, and planning time—and defend it.

Common trap: Many business owners spend 80% of their week delivering client work and 0% on filling the next pipeline. Then panic hits. A Commercial Director always reserves time to work *on* the business, not just *in* it.

5. Build with the End in Mind

Commercial Directors think beyond the week. They understand where the business is heading:

- Do we want to scale?
- Do we want freedom?
- Do we want to exit?

This clarity shapes daily decisions. If your goal is recurring income, you'll turn down tempting one-offs. If your aim is lifestyle, you'll build lean and automate early. If it's a sale, you'll document every process for future buyers.

Future-focus question: What decisions are you making today that will pay off in 12 months?

If you can't answer that, you're not thinking like a Commercial Director yet.

Building the Commercial Toolkit

To make the mindset stick, you need tools and systems that reinforce it.

Here are five practical components of a Commercial Director's toolkit that can be adapted for any business size:

1. Weekly Commercial Review Template

This template should include:

- Revenue performance (week-on-week and month-to-date)
- Lead flow volume and source
- Sales conversion metrics
- Pipeline forecast
- Campaign performance

- Blockers and opportunities

Tip: Run this review every Monday. Don't delegate it. This is your cockpit.

2. Revenue Impact Matrix

Use a 2x2 matrix to evaluate every idea:

- X-axis: Effort
- Y-axis: Impact

Plot your marketing, content, partnerships, product ideas—then prioritise those in the top-right quadrant (high impact, low effort). This removes emotion and forces focus.

3. Revenue Dashboard (Live or Manual)

Track:

- Top-line revenue
- Revenue by product/service
- Recurring vs one-off
- Average deal size
- Cost per lead
- ROI by channel

Even a Google Sheet is better than nothing. What matters is visibility.

4. Leverage Calendar

List your high-leverage commercial actions for each week. For example:

- Book 3 follow-up calls
- Record 1 nurture video

- Contact 1 past client
- Re-engage 1 lost lead

Doing 5 of these per week compounds massively over time.

5. Delegation Framework

Use the DAD model:

- **Do:** Tasks only you can do
- **Automate:** Tasks that repeat
- **Delegate:** Everything else

Most founders hang onto low-leverage work out of habit. You can't think commercially if your time is spent on admin.

Sector Examples: How This Mindset Applies Across Industries

1. Digital Marketing Agency Challenge: Feast-and-famine sales, founder trapped in delivery. Commercial Shift:

- Documented onboarding and delivery processes
- Dedicated 2 hours/week to new business
- Scaled lead gen via webinars and case study content Result: Doubled MRR in 6 months.

2. Construction Trades Firm Challenge: No repeat business, reliant on lead ads. Commercial Shift:

- Introduced service contracts
- Mapped and optimised referral system
- CRM to track lead sources and sales stages Result: 3x customer retention, reduced ad spend by 40%.

3. Coaching Consultant Challenge: Unpredictable income, no lead tracking. Commercial Shift:

- Clarified offer into fixed packages
- Used LinkedIn to attract ideal clients
- Weekly commercial scorecard and reflection Result: 50% increase in conversions, consistent pipeline.

4. Local Retail Business Challenge: Slow walk-in traffic, no digital strategy. Commercial Shift:

- Introduced click-and-collect and email marketing
- Reviewed local SEO and Google My Business weekly
- Set target for customer reviews and referral incentives Result: 20% increase in store visits, 30% increase in online sales.

The Commercial Leadership Shift: From Firefighter to Strategist

As a founder or senior leader, you may currently be:

- Reacting to problems instead of solving root causes
- Jumping from sales to delivery without pause
- Measuring success emotionally, not commercially

Stepping into Commercial Director thinking changes all that.

You move from:

- Panic to planning
- Random to rhythm
- Volume to value
- Confusion to clarity

This shift doesn't happen overnight. But it happens every time you:

- Block time for thinking

- Hold yourself accountable to numbers
- Ask better questions before taking action
- Build systems that support success

Your Commercial Habits (Daily, Weekly, Monthly)

Daily:

- Review numbers and top 3 priorities
- Reconnect with one commercial contact
- Make one offer, pitch, or follow-up

Weekly:

- Run the commercial review
- Reflect on what worked, what didn't, and why
- Delegate one task you've held onto too long

Monthly:

- Review all revenue sources and margins
- Set a new experiment (e.g., offer, content, process)
- Realign your calendar with your commercial goals

Over time, these habits define your role—and your results.

Final Thought: Lead Like the Director Your Business Deserves

You don't need to be hired into this role. You already have it. Your business needs a leader who:

- Thinks commercially
- Plans strategically
- Acts with focus

- Measures with honesty
- Adapts with clarity

This isn't corporate. This is critical.

The Commercial Director mindset doesn't make you cold or rigid. It makes you sharper, calmer, and more effective. It protects your energy, aligns your efforts, and keeps the business growing—even when you're not in the room.

Step into it fully.

Your future business will thank you.

CHAPTER 13

How to Lead a Marketing Team

In many businesses, marketing is treated like a bolt-on—an afterthought, a service function, or worse, a department to blame when leads don't land. But marketing isn't a service you outsource and forget about. It's a crucial engine in your commercial machine. And if you're going to lead it—whether it's one freelancer, an agency, or a full in-house team—you need to know how to do it well.

This chapter is about **how to lead marketers**—creatives, strategists, copywriters, designers, and digital specialists—not how to do their jobs. You don't need to write every caption or design every graphic. But you do need to guide the direction, hold standards, and make sure everything aligns with your commercial goals.

If you're the business owner, founder, director, or someone managing marketing as part of your role, this chapter will show you exactly how to:

- Set clear expectations for marketing performance
- Lead creative personalities without micromanaging
- Build structure, feedback, and rhythm into your campaigns
- Align marketing with sales, delivery, and business strategy
- Create momentum, trust, and results without chaos

You don't need to be a marketing expert to lead a team well. You just need to lead with purpose. Let's break it down.

The Role of Leadership in Marketing

Before we get into the practical structures of how to lead marketers, it's important to acknowledge the unique challenge many business owners face: leading in a space you didn't train in.

You might not have a marketing degree. You might not have worked as a copywriter, SEO strategist, or digital campaign manager. And that's OK. You don't need to become the expert in every channel—but you do need to become a **leader of experts**.

Leading a marketing team is less about having the answers and more about asking the right questions. It's about seeing the bigger picture, identifying the blind spots, and helping the team focus on what really moves the needle. Marketing requires a balance of empathy and edge. You're dealing with creative, often sensitive personalities who thrive on ideas and experimentation. But you're also accountable to commercial performance.

Too many leaders fall into one of two traps:

1. **They become too hands-off**, assuming marketing will "just handle it". The result? Disconnected campaigns, misaligned messaging, and wasted spend.

2. **They become too controlling**, rewriting every post and micromanaging every campaign. The result? A demotivated team, stale output, and missed opportunities for innovation.

Your job is to sit firmly in the middle: involved, but not invasive. Strategic, but not stifling. Curious, but not controlling. Let's explore what that looks like in practice.

Let's get something straight: leading a marketing team is not the same as leading a sales team. Marketing people are wired differently. Their work is often less tangible in the short term, more creative in nature, and open to interpretation. That means your leadership approach needs to be tuned accordingly.

Too many business owners lead marketers like project managers: "Did you post the blog? Did the email go out? How many likes did we get?" But that's not leadership—it's oversight. Great marketing leadership means:

- Giving direction, not dictation
- Setting clear goals, not vague hopes
- Creating space for creativity, but within structure
- Holding people accountable without crushing momentum

Your job is not to tell marketers *how* to do every job—it's to make sure they know *why* they're doing it, *who* it's for, and *what* success looks like.

Mindset Shift: From Output to Outcome

Let's bring this to life with a few more examples:

B2B Professional Services: A consultancy firm was publishing LinkedIn content 4–5 times a week. They saw good engagement but couldn't link a single piece of content to new client enquiries. We introduced a single monthly campaign framework: each month would focus on one key service, supported by relevant posts, webinars, and client stories. Engagement dipped slightly—but inbound leads doubled within 60 days.

E-commerce Brand: A direct-to-consumer fitness product company was pouring money into Facebook ads. Clicks were high, but conversion was poor. When we aligned the ad messaging with post-purchase onboarding and email follow-ups that reinforced the offer and value, the average order value increased by 28%.

The point? When your marketers understand how their work fits into the bigger commercial puzzle, they stop producing noise—and start producing results.

Marketers often get buried in outputs: social posts, campaigns, email designs, landing pages. But output doesn't equal outcome.

Your leadership must centre on commercial outcomes:

- Are we generating leads?
- Are we increasing conversion?
- Are we building brand trust in our market?
- Are we supporting the sales process?

When your team knows that the goal isn't "post more" but "drive results," their priorities shift—and so does your marketing.

Real example: One company I worked with was producing two blog posts a week, posting daily on Instagram, and sending out a fortnightly newsletter. Lots of activity. But none of it was linked to sales conversations, product launches, or lead nurturing. Once we refocused efforts around a single commercial campaign each month—tied to one product or service—the results skyrocketed. Engagement went down, but conversion went up. That's the power of outcome-focused leadership.

Building a High-Functioning Marketing Rhythm

Case example: One of our clients, a regional B2B service provider, was working with a remote marketing assistant and a freelance designer. Work was constantly last-minute. Assets arrived hours before deadlines.

Campaigns were missed due to misunderstandings. We introduced a simple weekly 20-minute Monday meeting and a shared Google calendar with campaign dates mapped six weeks in advance. Within one quarter, their campaign delivery rate went from 62% to 94%. Response rates improved, and the internal stress dropped dramatically.

Rhythm breeds results.

Great marketing teams don't work in chaos. They work in rhythm.

You need to create predictable patterns of work, feedback, and improvement:

- Weekly check-ins (15–30 minutes)
- Monthly performance reviews
- Quarterly planning sessions
- Campaign retrospectives

These aren't meetings for the sake of it. They create:

- Focus
- Alignment
- Accountability
- Space for creativity

Without rhythm, everything feels last-minute. Content becomes reactive. Messaging gets diluted. Teams burn out. Results stall.

Framework:

- Monday: Review last week's performance, set priorities
- Wednesday: Midweek sync or approvals
- Friday: Content scheduled, pipeline reviewed, key learnings noted

That's leadership through structure—not control.

Managing Internal, External, and Hybrid Teams

Marketing leadership looks different depending on who's doing the work:

- **In-house marketers** (employees): need clear KPIs, development plans, and visibility.

- **Freelancers**: need briefs, timelines, approvals, and payment clarity.
- **Agencies**: need commercial direction, brand understanding, and consistent communication.

Tips for all three:

- Have one clear point of contact
- Define the core message and goals every quarter
- Build a shared calendar or campaign planner
- Review performance against agreed outcomes, not just deliverables

You can't just hand off marketing and hope for the best. You need to lead it. That means weekly communication, monthly reviews, and direct feedback—good or bad.

Golden rule: If your marketer doesn't know what your sales team is focused on, you've already failed.

Aligning Marketing With Sales and Delivery

One of the most powerful things you can do as a leader is to remove friction between departments. When marketing operates in isolation from sales and delivery, you get mismatched messaging, broken promises, and confused customers.

As the leader, your job is to create cross-functional clarity. That starts with aligning around a shared commercial goal.

Tactical Tip: Every month, host a joint session between your sales, marketing, and delivery teams. Get answers to these questions:

- What's our key product/service focus this quarter?
- What questions are prospects asking that marketing can answer?

- What's causing friction in delivery that sales can set better expectations around?
- What campaigns can support current revenue targets?

This isn't about creating bureaucracy—it's about building flow. Everyone should understand the full buyer journey and their role in it.

Example: A coaching business I worked with found that marketing was promising "rapid transformation," but the delivery team knew that sustainable client results took 90 days. This disconnect led to dropouts. When we adjusted the campaign language and added a new onboarding explainer, retention increased by 37%.

Setting Standards Without Killing Creativity

Marketing is inherently creative. But that doesn't mean it should be chaotic.

You need to set standards—not to limit expression, but to sharpen it. These standards fall into three categories:

1. **Brand** – Fonts, colours, voice, tone, visuals.
2. **Message** – Core themes, values, offers, differentiation.
3. **Quality** – Spelling, structure, clarity, visual consistency.

Make your expectations known early. Don't assume your team knows what "on-brand" means to you.

Create a living document—your brand playbook. It doesn't have to be a polished PDF.

A shared Google Doc that outlines:

- Core brand colours and logo usage
- Voice of tone ("straight-talking," "friendly," "no fluff," etc.)
- Key audience personas
- What's in scope, what's not

This creates creative freedom *within boundaries*—the sweet spot where the best marketing lives.

Feedback That Builds, Not Breaks

One of the most common complaints I hear from marketing teams is this:

"I get vague, conflicting, or last-minute feedback."

Good feedback is structured, timely, and tied to outcomes. Here's how to give feedback that builds momentum:

1. Be specific. Bad: "This post doesn't feel right." Better: "Let's tie this back to our core pain point: inconsistent sales."

2. Be timely. Waiting until launch day to give input kills trust. Review drafts early.

3. Be strategic. Don't just react to what *you* like—focus on what the *audience* needs.

4. Use a format. Try this:

- What worked well?
- What needs refining?
- Is it aligned with the goal?
- What's the next step?

Pro tip: If you find yourself rewriting your marketer's work entirely, the problem might be the brief—not the execution.

Marketing KPIs That Matter

As a leader, you need to track what matters. That doesn't mean obsessing over every data point—but you do need a small set of key metrics to guide decisions.

Here's a practical set of KPIs by category:

Content/Engagement

- Reach (views, impressions)
- Click-through rate
- Email open rate

Lead Generation

- Number of leads per channel
- Cost per lead (if paid)
- Form conversion rate

Sales Alignment

- Sales-qualified leads (SQLs)
- Lead-to-close ratio
- Time from lead to sale

Revenue Impact

- Marketing-sourced revenue
- ROI per campaign
- Customer lifetime value (CLV)

Use a simple dashboard. Even a Google Sheet updated weekly or monthly can keep the team focused.

Remember: Numbers aren't there to punish—they're there to learn from. Every metric tells a story. As the leader, it's your job to help your team interpret it.

Delegating Without Losing Control

One of the biggest fears leaders have when managing marketing teams is that if they step back, the quality will drop. That fear creates micromanagement. Micromanagement creates resentment. Resentment kills creativity.

You don't have to choose between being involved and being hands-off. The right approach is structured delegation:

1. Delegate outcomes, not just tasks. Instead of "Write a blog post on topic X," say: "Create a piece of content that helps our audience understand why X is hurting their results—and positions us as the solution."

2. Give clear constraints. Deadlines, tone, CTA, length—give the rules of the game upfront so your team has space to play, but within a framework.

3. Trust the process. If your team or agency has delivered well in the past, let them run the process—then give feedback once it's 80% done. Don't kill momentum at 20%.

4. Review regularly. A 30-minute weekly touchpoint keeps small issues from becoming big ones.

5. Celebrate wins. Recognition drives motivation. When a campaign lands, share the credit. When a team member levels up, let them know it's seen.

Real-world example: One founder I worked with had a part-time marketing assistant who was capable, but underperforming. The founder was doing all the rewrites herself and felt like she couldn't let go. We introduced a clearer content brief template and a rule: the assistant would draft fully, and the founder would only review after the second round. Within six weeks, the assistant was hitting the mark with minimal changes. That founder didn't lower her standards—she raised her clarity. Delegation worked because the rules were clear and the outcome was owned.

Leading Through Change

Marketing is one of the fastest-moving parts of your business. Tools evolve. Platforms change. Audience attention shifts. If you're not careful, your team can burn out chasing every trend or stall out waiting for you to decide.

One of my clients, a consumer brand heavily reliant on Instagram, was caught flat-footed when Meta's algorithm update tanked their organic reach. Engagement fell by 70% in a month. Panic set in.

The internal conversation turned to "What platform do we jump to next?" Instead, we paused and reviewed the long-term strategy. We focused on improving email nurturing, launching a weekly newsletter, and investing in retargeting ads. Within 90 days, they'd not only recovered lost sales—they'd diversified their lead sources and were no longer at the mercy of one algorithm.

As a leader, you need to be:

- A signal in the noise
- A calm in the chaos
- A strategic voice when everyone's focused on tactics

Here's how:

1. Embrace the 70/20/10 Rule.

- 70% of marketing should be what's proven to work.
- 20% should be iterative improvements.
- 10% can be experimental (new platforms, formats, campaigns).

2. Be transparent about priorities. Change is fine. Surprise change is not. Give your team a heads-up when goals shift.

3. Balance urgency with vision. Campaigns matter. But so does brand. Push for short-term wins without compromising long-term trust.

4. Model commercial thinking. Don't ask for more content—ask for smarter content. Ask: "What's the purpose of this?" before "What does it look like?"

Marketing is one of the fastest-moving parts of your business. Tools evolve. Platforms change. Audience attention shifts. If you're not careful, your team can burn out chasing every trend or stall out waiting for you to decide.

You don't need to be the most creative person in the room. You need to be the most commercially aware. You need to set the bar, keep the direction, and build the conditions for great work to thrive.

Because when marketing is led well—it doesn't just produce content. It drives growth, builds brand equity, and fuels the entire commercial engine.

And when it's aligned, empowered, and accountable? That's when marketing becomes a multiplier—not a cost.

Lead it like that—and your whole business shifts.

CHAPTER 14

The Invisible Drain on Your Sales

It's not your pitch. It's not your product. It's not even your pricing.

The biggest threat to your revenue isn't usually the thing you're obsessing over.

It's the stuff you're not seeing. The missed follow-ups. The weak handovers. The forgotten proposals. The cold leads sitting in your CRM while your team chases shiny new ones.

This is the invisible drain on your sales—and it's costing you more than you think.

In this chapter, we're going to uncover the silent killers of your pipeline and show you how to:

- Spot the leaks that are killing conversion
- Fix the gaps between marketing and sales
- Stop losing deals you should have closed
- Build a system that captures, tracks, and converts consistently

Because the truth is, most businesses don't need more leads. They need to stop wasting the ones they've already paid for.

The Leaks You Can't Afford to Ignore

Let's start with a painful truth: every business is leaking sales. Even the good ones.

What separates the winners from the strugglers isn't the ability to generate leads—it's the ability to convert and retain them.

The Glue

Here are the most common invisible drains we see:

1. No Follow-Up System Leads come in, maybe get a call, and then… nothing. No second contact. No value sent. No structured sequence. You wouldn't believe how many businesses think one touchpoint is enough. It's not. Most sales happen between the 5th and 12th touch.

2. Disconnected Marketing and Sales Marketing sends leads that sales says are "rubbish." Sales ignores leads because there's no context. The handover is broken—or worse, non-existent.

3. Slow Response Time A lead submits a form. It takes someone two days to respond. By then, they've spoken to your competitor.

4. Weak Qualification Your team is wasting hours on leads that were never a fit. No filters, no scoring, no clear criteria.

5. No Pipeline Visibility Your team has no idea who's where in the buying journey. Leads live in inboxes, spreadsheets, or forgotten corners of a CRM.

Each of these leaks, left unchecked, creates compounding damage. Not only are you missing revenue—you're burning your team's energy, wasting marketing spend, and damaging brand trust.

Leak #1: No Follow-Up System

This is the most common—and costly—drain in almost every business. Leads arrive. You respond. Maybe there's a conversation. And then… silence.

Follow-up is where the majority of sales are won or lost. It's not the first email or call—it's the second, third, or fourth where trust is built, questions get answered, and objections get cleared.

Why this happens:

- No clear ownership of the follow-up process
- No CRM automation or reminders

- No content assets to support follow-up

The fix:

- Set a follow-up standard: Minimum 5 attempts over 10 days
- Build a follow-up library: case studies, testimonials, FAQs, product sheets
- Use automation tools (like HubSpot, Pipedrive, or even Calendly reminders) to prompt timely action

Real-world example: One of our clients, a B2B tech consultancy, was sending proposals and then hoping for the best. We implemented a 5-touchpoint sequence that included calls, emails, and two value-add pieces of content. Their proposal-to-close rate increased from 24% to 41% in 60 days.

Leak #2: Disconnected Marketing and Sales

Marketing generates leads. Sales tries to close them. But if these two teams aren't aligned on what a good lead looks like, how the lead got there, and what context the buyer already has—it's like running a relay with no baton pass.

Symptoms:

- Sales ignoring marketing-qualified leads
- Marketing judged by lead volume instead of quality
- No feedback loop between teams

The fix:

- Hold a monthly alignment session between marketing and sales
- Define a shared lead scoring model (what counts as warm, cold, sales-ready)
- Give sales visibility of lead journey: what content they've seen, forms filled, emails clicked

Tactical tip: Use a shared dashboard (Google Data Studio, CRM reports) that both teams can see and update in real time.

Leak #3: Slow Response Time

Speed matters. A Harvard Business Review study found that businesses that respond to leads within an hour are 7x more likely to qualify that lead. Yet most businesses take 24–48 hours to reply.

What's causing the delay?

- No notification system
- Manual handovers
- Leads submitted outside office hours and no automation to pick them up

Solutions:

- Use autoresponders that confirm receipt and set expectations
- Route new leads instantly via email, Slack, or SMS
- Use tools like Calendly to let prospects book directly

Example: One client added a booking link to their contact form confirmation page and saw a 37% increase in booked calls overnight.

Leak #4: Weak Qualification

Not all leads are worth pursuing. But if you don't qualify effectively, you waste hours on the wrong ones—and miss the hot ones.

Signs of poor qualification:

- Sales reps asking basic discovery questions that could have been on the form
- Marketing sending every lead as "warm"
- Inconsistent lead scoring

Your fix:

- Add qualification fields to your forms (budget, timeline, challenge)
- Introduce a lead scoring model based on firmographic data and behaviour
- Train sales teams to tier leads: A, B, C—each with a different follow-up plan

Tool tip: Use conditional logic in your forms (like Typeform or Gravity Forms) to segment and sort leads automatically.

Leak #5: No Pipeline Visibility

If you can't see your leads, you can't close them. Simple as that. Many businesses still rely on fragmented spreadsheets, disconnected inboxes, or outdated CRMs. When you can't see your pipeline, you can't manage it.

Symptoms:

- You don't know how many active leads are in your funnel right now
- Follow-ups are missed because people forget where the lead left off
- No clarity on how many deals are in each stage of the sales process

The fix:

- Set up a CRM (even if it's basic): HubSpot Free, Pipedrive, Popcorn, Trello—just pick one
- Define your sales stages: New Lead > Contacted > Qualified > Proposal > Closed Won/Lost
- Review your pipeline every week—what's moving forward, what's stuck, and why

Real-world example: One of our consultancy clients was working off email threads and notes on paper. We built a Trello board with each sales stage as a column. Within two weeks, their entire team had visibility, collaboration improved, and deals stopped falling through the cracks. It wasn't about the tool—it was about the habit of working the pipeline like a process.

Fixing the System: From Reactive to Revenue-Driven

Now that we've covered the five major invisible drains, let's talk about plugging the holes and building a commercial system that works.

What we're aiming for is simple:

- Clear processes
- Trackable metrics
- Sales and marketing alignment
- Consistent follow-up
- A pipeline that builds momentum

This is what separates scalable businesses from ones that flatline.

Let's build it.

Step 1: Map the Journey

Every business should have a mapped-out customer journey. Not just the stages of the funnel, but what happens at each one.

Here's a basic flow:

1. Awareness: Prospect hears about you
2. Engagement: Prospect interacts (clicks, downloads, attends)
3. Qualification: Prospect is vetted and scored
4. Conversion: Proposal sent or purchase made
5. Delivery: Onboarding, service, retention

Ask yourself:

- Do you know what content or campaign drives each stage?
- Do your teams know their responsibilities at each stage?
- Do your systems track movement from one stage to the next?

If not—fix that first.

Step 2: Build Lead Management Discipline

Lead discipline is about what happens the moment a lead appears.

- Who owns it?
- When are they contacted?
- What's the first thing they receive?
- What happens after that?

Create rules that everyone understands:

- All leads are responded to within 2 hours
- All leads are entered into the CRM
- Every lead has a next step logged
- Unresponsive leads are followed up 5 times minimum

This isn't hard—it just needs leadership.

Step 3: Create a Handoff Protocol

One of the biggest breakdowns in most sales pipelines is the transition from marketing to sales. A lead fills out a form, downloads a guide, or attends a webinar—then sits in limbo while sales figures out what to do next. This moment matters.

A clean handoff builds momentum. A messy one kills it.

Build a simple handoff process:

- A single point of contact logs the lead into the CRM

- Lead owner is assigned immediately
- A short summary of lead behaviour is added (what they clicked, downloaded, etc.)
- A templated intro email is sent

Bonus tip: Use automation to prefill this info into your CRM notes. Tools like Zapier can grab form fields and populate the right data instantly.

Step 4: Use Templates to Speed Execution

Speed doesn't mean cutting corners—it means removing unnecessary thinking time. Every team needs a small library of go-to templates:

- Follow-up emails (day 1, 3, 5, 10, etc.)
- Call scripts for discovery and qualification
- Proposal templates with modifiable blocks
- Objection-handling responses

Don't over-engineer it. Just make sure your team never starts from a blank page.

Step 5: Track the Right Numbers

You don't need a 20-tab dashboard. But you do need a few numbers that show whether your pipeline is healthy:

- Lead-to-contact rate
- Contact-to-qualified rate
- Qualified-to-proposal rate
- Proposal-to-close rate
- Average days to close

If you track those weekly, you'll catch issues early. You'll know where the drop-off is. You'll know whether it's a lead issue, a sales issue, or a follow-up issue.

Final Checklist: Patch the Leaks and Power the Pipeline

Use this checklist to audit your business right now. Tick off what's in place—and highlight what needs action.

Follow-Up

- Do you have a minimum follow-up sequence?
- Are follow-ups tracked and logged?
- Do you have assets to support follow-up (case studies, FAQs)?

Marketing and Sales Alignment

- Do both teams agree on lead quality definitions?
- Are campaigns reviewed together?
- Is there a regular feedback loop?

Speed to Lead

- Are leads contacted within 2 hours?
- Is there an automated first response?
- Can leads book directly into your calendar?

Qualification

- Do your forms capture the right information?
- Is there a clear scoring system?
- Are leads tiered into hot/warm/cold buckets?

Pipeline Visibility

- Is your CRM up to date?
- Can you see every lead's stage?
- Is the pipeline reviewed weekly?

Systems and Templates

- Do you have proposal and follow-up templates?
- Is your handoff process documented?
- Are key numbers being tracked weekly?

Fixing your invisible drains isn't a one-time event. It's a habit. But when you get it right, everything changes:

- Sales becomes predictable
- Marketing becomes more effective
- Your team wastes less time
- You close more of the leads you already have

The best growth doesn't come from doing more. It comes from stopping the waste.

This chapter wasn't about generating leads. It was about respecting the ones you've got.

Plug the leaks. Protect your pipeline. And watch your sales rise—without spending a penny more on lead gen.

CHAPTER 15

Build It Around Your Life

We don't start businesses just to be busy.

We don't hire teams, win clients, and build brands so we can work 80 hours a week, miss our kids' milestones, and burn out before the business even gets off the ground.

But that's exactly what happens to most business owners.

They become trapped in the very thing they created. They trade one job for another—and this one doesn't even come with sick pay.

This chapter is about building your business around your life—not the other way around.

Because growth means nothing if it costs you everything.

And your marketing and sales strategy? It should reflect that.

If you want a business that's sustainable, scalable, and supports your actual goals—not just your revenue targets—then you need to rethink how you structure it.

You need to lead it. Shape it. Design it.

Not drift into it.

So let's talk about how you do that.

Let's talk about building it around your life.

The Myth of Hustle

Let's start with the lie we've all been sold: that the more hours you work, the more successful you'll be. Hustle culture, rise-and-grind

Instagram quotes, and business gurus tell us that sleep is for the weak and that we should wear burnout like a badge of honour.

But here's the truth:

Burnout doesn't build businesses. It breaks them.

You can't sell clearly, think creatively, or lead effectively when you're permanently knackered.

The people who build successful, sustainable businesses aren't the ones sprinting endlessly. They're the ones who've designed the game to work around their energy, their values, and their life.

You don't need to work 18-hour days to prove your commitment. You need a structure that allows you to show up at your best.

That's what this chapter is about.

What Does 'Life-First Business' Actually Mean?

This isn't about working less for the sake of it. It's about aligning your business with your personal priorities so that both thrive.

A life-first business means:

- You protect time for your family, health, and recovery
- Your model supports your income goals without maxing out your calendar
- You choose clients and projects that energise you, not just pay you
- You say no more often than yes—and you do it guilt-free

Step 1: Decide What 'Life' Looks Like First

You can't build a business around your life until you define what that life looks like.

Start by answering these questions:

- What do your ideal weekdays look like?

- When do you want to start and finish work?
- How many hours a week do you want to work?
- What are the non-negotiables in your personal life (family dinners, school runs, gym time)?
- What energises you—and what drains you?

Too many people build businesses without ever asking these questions. They build a business that demands more than they're willing to give—and then resent it when it succeeds.

Let's fix that.

Step 2: Audit Your Model

Once you've defined the life you want, you need to ask: is your current business model supporting that?

If your model only works when you're working 60+ hours a week—it's broken.

Audit:

- Your pricing: Are you charging enough to cover both time and value?
- Your offer: Are you selling a service that scales or one that traps you?
- Your delivery: Is it reliant on you, or can others deliver it?
- Your marketing: Is it generating leads without your constant input?
- Your sales: Is it predictable—or based on your availability and energy?

A sustainable model is one that works **when you do—and when you don't.**

Step 3: Rebuild Your Calendar

The clearest way to see whether you're building a life-first business is to look at your calendar. Does it reflect your priorities—or everyone else's?

Start with this principle: **Protect your best energy for your best work.**

If your most productive hours are in the morning, block those out for strategy, deep work, or selling—not admin, firefighting, or back-to-back meetings.

Tactical calendar moves:

- Block weekly non-negotiables (family, exercise, creative time)
- Group meetings into blocks (e.g. Tuesday/Thursday only)
- Keep at least one day a week meeting-free
- Pre-book personal time like holidays, school plays, or down days before your diary fills up

Remember: Your calendar isn't just a tool—it's your boundary system. It either protects your energy or leaks it.

Step 4: Build a Business That Doesn't Rely on You

This is the real lever.

If your business falls apart when you take a day off, it's not a business—it's a job with overheads.

You don't have to become completely hands-off. But you do need to:

- Delegate delivery to people who can uphold your standards
- Automate lead nurturing and booking processes
- Systemise repeatable tasks
- Hire for support before you need it—not after you burn out

Real example: One business owner I worked with hadn't taken a proper holiday in three years. Every proposal, every sales call, every onboarding email went through them. We identified the 10 tasks that ate up 60% of their week and built simple systems for each—templates, training, and delegation. Within 90 days, they took their first 10-day break without their phone.

Freedom isn't found. It's built.

Step 5: Set Financial Targets That Support Your Life

Revenue is a vanity metric if it doesn't serve your real goals.

Don't just chase 7-figure targets because the internet says you should. Set income goals based on the life you want to live—how much it costs to live well, save, invest, and create freedom.

Ask yourself:

- What do I actually need to earn to support the lifestyle I want?
- What does financial peace of mind look like?
- How much buffer do I need to say no to bad-fit clients?
- Then build backwards:
- How many clients do you need at your current pricing?
- What's your average sales cycle?
- Where does your best lead flow come from?

Now your marketing and sales strategy becomes a tool to support your life—not just a machine for growth at all costs.

Step 6: Choose Clients Who Fit Your Life

You don't just need clients who pay well—you need clients who respect your time, energy, and values.

This is about fit. The best clients:

- Respect your boundaries

- Communicate clearly
- Follow your process
- Pay on time

You get to decide who you work with. But only if you're willing to say no.

Saying yes to bad-fit clients will cost you far more than the revenue is worth—it'll drain your energy, delay better opportunities, and anchor your business to a version of yourself you no longer want to be.

Your sales process should be selective. Let people opt out. Let your marketing repel the wrong people as much as it attracts the right ones.

This is how you build with intention.

Final Step: Design for Your Energy, Not Just Your Time

We're used to managing time. But the real differentiator in your business isn't your schedule—it's your **energy**.

Some tasks drain you. Some give you energy back. A business that's built around your life accounts for both.

Ask:

- What tasks leave you energised?
- What types of work leave you feeling flat?
- What environments bring out your best thinking?
- Who in your world drains your energy—and who lifts it?

Redesign your week with energy in mind:

- Batch high-energy tasks together
- Schedule deep work after rest, not after a sprint of meetings
- Protect mental recovery—walks, breaks, unplugged time

You're not a robot. And you're not a resource. You're the engine of your business.

Look after the engine.

Your Life-First Business Checklist

Use this as a gut-check every 90 days:

Life Clarity

- I've defined what my ideal week looks like
- I know what matters most to me outside of work

Model Fit

- My pricing supports my financial needs
- My offer can scale or flex with my time
- I have recurring or leveraged revenue in place

Time & Energy

- My calendar reflects my best hours and personal priorities
- I have at least one meeting-free day per week
- I'm protecting recovery and space

Systems & Support

- I have automation for leads and sales
- I've delegated delivery or admin tasks
- I have support in place before crisis hits

Client Fit

- I work only with clients who align with my values
- I say no to opportunities that compromise my life

This is how you build a business around your life—not just around the next month's revenue.

You're allowed to want more. More ease. More alignment. More joy.

And you're allowed to build for it.

Summary: Build Intentionally, Live Fully

- Hustle is not a badge of honour—burnout is not a business strategy
- Start by defining the life you actually want, then build the business to match
- Audit your model, your calendar, your systems, and your pricing
- Protect your energy as fiercely as your revenue
- Choose clients who respect your boundaries
- Use systems to support—not trap—you

Because business isn't just about growth. It's about freedom. It's about creating something that supports the life you want to live.

And that starts by building it on purpose. Not by default. Not by accident.

On purpose—and around your life.

PART 4

Presence & Power

CHAPTER 16

Visibility is Your Job

If no one knows who you are, no one can buy from you.

Simple—but powerful.

We spend so much time behind screens, scheduling content, tweaking funnels, and refining copy that we forget one of the oldest and most effective rules in business:

People buy from people they know, like, and trust.

And that trust isn't just built through digital channels. It's built in the real world—face to face, handshake to handshake, conversation by conversation.

This chapter is about visibility. Not social media visibility. Real visibility.

In the room. On the floor. At the front.

Whether you're at a networking event, hosting a workshop, shaking hands after a keynote, or chatting over coffee—you are the brand.

This chapter will show you:

- Why in-person presence builds trust faster than any ad campaign
- How to become known in your local or industry ecosystem
- The value of networking when done with intent (not just small talk)
- Why your job isn't just to lead—but to be *seen* leading

- How I've used Hashtag Events and consistent presence to generate inbound leads, referrals, and long-term opportunity

This is the chapter that brings sales and marketing into the flesh. No algorithms. No paid ads. Just people, presence, and positioning.

Let's get you seen.

The Visibility Gap

You can have the best offer in the world, but if you're not visible, none of it matters.

There's a gap between how good your business is—and how many people know about it. That's the visibility gap. And it's the reason some mediocre businesses scale fast while brilliant ones stay stuck.

Visibility isn't just marketing's job. It's yours.

As the founder, business owner, or leader—you *are* the most powerful ambassador of your brand. Not your content. Not your team. You.

This doesn't mean you need to be everywhere, all the time. It means you need to choose *where* you'll show up—and own it.

In a room full of decision-makers, buyers, and collaborators—your presence speaks louder than any brochure.

This is why offline presence matters. It's not old school. It's high-impact. And most people are avoiding it because it takes effort, vulnerability, and consistency.

That's your advantage.

Why Offline Still Wins

We live in a digital-first world. But trust is still built fastest when people can look you in the eye, read your energy, and shake your hand.

Offline wins because:

- It's harder to fake

- It creates deeper memory recall
- It builds stronger emotional connection
- It allows immediate feedback, adaptation, and rapport

How many online connections have turned into real opportunities for you? Now ask—how many conversations in real life have led to a deal, a referral, or a long-term client?

Offline creates context. And context converts.

How to Get Seen (Strategically)

You don't need to attend every event or network with everyone. You need a plan. Here's how to get visible with intention:

1. Choose Your Rooms Not all events are equal. Find the places where your ideal clients, partners, or referrers show up. That could be local business events, trade shows, charity fundraisers, or niche expos.

2. Show Up Consistently One-off appearances rarely build traction. You need to be seen regularly enough that people associate you with your field. Repetition builds recognition. Recognition builds trust.

3. Be Memorable, Not Salesy You don't need a pitch. You need a presence. Be clear about what you do, who you help, and what makes you different—but never lead with the hard sell.

4. Use Follow-Up as a Visibility Tool The first interaction is only the beginning. The follow-up is where relationships form. Send a personal message. Share a relevant resource. Invite to connect. Don't sell—just stay present.

5. Document, Don't Promote Use LinkedIn or your platform of choice to document where you've been, what you've learned, or who you've connected with. It keeps you top of mind—without needing to shout.

Real-World Example: Hashtag Events

I've worked with Hashtag Events for years—as an ambassador, speaker, and partner.

Why? Because they've created the perfect environment for visibility.

Their events aren't just trade shows—they're high-energy networking ecosystems. Rooms full of decision-makers, entrepreneurs, marketers, and salespeople. And importantly—real people having real conversations.

At one Hashtag event, I delivered a short workshop on aligning sales and marketing. After the session, a local business owner approached me to talk about their struggles with disjointed lead flow. That conversation led to a consulting contract that's now in its third year. Not because I pushed a pitch—but because I showed up, gave value, and followed up with purpose.

In another instance, a connection made during a casual coffee at a Hashtag breakfast event turned into a speaking invitation, which then led to referrals from the attendees of that talk. One room created ripple effects that spanned across multiple quarters of inbound leads.

By showing up consistently:

- I've had inbound leads from people who saw me speak
- Built relationships with business owners who refer me years later
- Grown brand awareness without paying for ads
- Seen clients close business simply by being seen in the right room

Command the Front of the Room

Visibility isn't just about showing up. It's about standing out. And one of the fastest ways to elevate your positioning is to take the mic.

The Glue

Whether it's a keynote, a panel slot, a 10-minute intro at a networking breakfast—being at the front of the room gives you instant credibility.

You become the expert.

And here's the secret: you don't need to be the most polished speaker. You just need to speak with clarity, conviction, and authenticity.

One of my clients—an SEO consultant—was hesitant to speak publicly but agreed to do a short session at a small local business expo. She spoke honestly about what most business owners get wrong about SEO. Her talk wasn't flashy—but it was clear, practical, and full of value. Within a week, she'd booked two new clients who had been in the room. Six months later, she was invited to speak at a regional conference. The turning point? She got visible at the front of the room.

Tips for commanding the room:

- Share stories, not just information
- Speak directly to the problems your audience actually cares about
- Invite interaction—make it a conversation, not a lecture
- Be generous with your value, not stingy with your pitch

When you speak well, people come to you. You shift from chasing leads to attracting them.

Visibility Routines That Work

Being visible doesn't have to mean draining your energy or calendar. Here's how to make it sustainable, with examples that work from my experience and my clients'.

Weekly:

- Attend one local networking event or business meetup. For example, I often visit smaller Hashtag-linked events midweek where the energy is more relaxed and the connections are high-quality.

- Post a recap or insight from that event online. A client of mine in the coaching space shares 3 key takeaways after each networking breakfast—positioning herself as reflective, professional, and connected.

- Follow up with 3–5 people you met. A quick message referencing your conversation goes a long way. One of my former clients booked a £7k project this way—with a simple, sincere follow-up email two days after meeting.

Monthly:

- Speak or host a session (even informally). I regularly run mini Q&A talks at local events. They don't take much prep—but they keep me visible and valuable.

- Visit a new room or event you haven't tried yet. One of my clients attended a local expo they'd previously ignored—and ended up with three new leads from a casual chat over coffee.

- Book in a coffee or lunch with a high-value contact. I make a point every month to reconnect in person with someone valuable in my network—not to sell, just to stay connected.

Quarterly:

- Sponsor or co-host an event. I've used quarterly partnerships with Hashtag Events to increase brand awareness—and it's led to inbound leads simply from having our name on the banner.

- Run a private workshop for your community. A consulting client of mine started doing this with just 6 attendees—and one turned into a long-term retainer deal.

- Review your visibility plan—what's working, what's not. I schedule one hour at the end of each quarter to look at visibility ROI—where I showed up, what impact it had, and what I need to double down on.

- Consistency wins. You don't need to do all of it. But you need to do *something*—and keep doing it.

Being visible doesn't have to mean draining your energy or calendar. Here's how to make it sustainable:

Weekly:

- Attend one local networking event or business meetup
- Post a recap or insight from that event online
- Follow up with 3–5 people you met

Monthly:

- Speak or host a session (even informally)
- Visit a new room or event you haven't tried yet
- Book in a coffee or lunch with a high-value contact

Quarterly:

- Sponsor or co-host an event
- Run a private workshop for your community
- Review your visibility plan—what's working, what's not

Consistency wins. You don't need to do all of it. But you need to do *something*—and keep doing it.

From Local Recognition to Industry Credibility

Visibility starts local. But when done right, it doesn't stop there.

You may begin by becoming known in your town, your region, your niche—but as your name becomes attached to value, reliability, and expertise, you'll find yourself being invited into rooms you never expected.

One example that stands out is a founder I worked with who started attending local networking breakfasts with zero profile and no public speaking experience. At first, he was just another face in the room. But he kept showing up—every month, without fail. He followed up with genuine interest, connected people with opportunities, and became a regular voice in discussions.

Six months later, he was asked to introduce a guest speaker. A few months after that, he was asked to host a panel. Today, he speaks regularly at industry events, has built a strong referral network, and gets consistent inbound leads—not because of a viral campaign, but because people trust what he's become known for. It started with visibility and scaled with consistency.

Start small. Stay consistent. Think big.

You don't need a national campaign to build authority. You need:

- Real conversations
- Real follow-up
- Real contribution

That's how your reputation compounds.

People will refer you because they've *seen* you show up—over and over again.

Visibility starts local. But when done right, it doesn't stop there.

You may begin by becoming known in your town, your region, your niche—but as your name becomes attached to value, reliability, and expertise, you'll find yourself being invited into rooms you never expected.

Summary: Presence Over Perfection

- If no one sees you, no one buys from you
- Visibility isn't just a marketing function—it's your leadership role
- Offline trust-building beats digital noise every time
- The rooms you enter shape the opportunities you attract
- Speaking positions you as the expert—fast
- Consistency, not volume, builds reputation

Visibility is a habit. A choice. A commercial superpower.

Get in the room. Be seen. Be remembered. Be trusted.

Because when you're the most visible person in your space—you become the most valuable.

CHAPTER 17

Be the Face of the Business

People don't buy from logos. They buy from people.

They don't connect with mission statements or marketing collateral. They connect with stories, personalities, and human presence.

And that means if you run the business—**you are the brand**.

You are the face they remember. You are the energy they trust. You are the reason they decide to buy, refer, return, or walk away.

This chapter is about stepping into that role with confidence and clarity. It's not about ego. It's not about fame. It's about *leadership*.

When people know who's behind the business, when they feel that presence consistently—in the room, on the call, in the content—they trust faster, engage deeper, and refer more confidently.

In this chapter, we'll cover:

- Why business owners must lead from the front
- How to show up with consistency without burning out
- Building a recognisable personal brand alongside the company brand
- How being the face of the business builds trust, sales, and scale

This isn't theory. This is practice. Let's make your presence a commercial asset.

Why the Face Matters More Than Ever

In a world where automation is everywhere and AI can write your emails, what sets you apart isn't your tech stack—it's your *humanity*.

People want to know who they're buying from. They want to know who's behind the scenes. They want to feel something when they interact with your brand—and that starts with you.

I once worked with a founder who had incredible testimonials, a brilliant website, and rock-solid credentials. But she remained anonymous—her name was buried in the footer, and her face never appeared on her LinkedIn or email campaigns. Conversion rates stayed flat. The moment she began sharing her personal story, using video in her outreach, and posting occasional insights into her day-to-day leadership, leads increased by 40% over three months. Her audience didn't change—her visibility did.

You can outsource content, design, delivery. But you can't outsource trust. You can't outsource credibility. And you absolutely can't outsource *presence*.

When a business has a visible, trusted face leading it, three things happen:

1. **Faster trust** – Prospects already feel like they know you before they ever speak to you.
2. **Stronger retention** – Clients stick because the relationship isn't just transactional—it's personal.
3. **Better referrals** – People don't say "go use XYZ Company." They say "you've got to speak to Gavin."

You don't need to be an influencer. But you do need to be *visible*. Because if you're invisible, you're forgettable.

And in today's market—forgettable is fatal.

In a world where automation is everywhere and AI can write your emails, what sets you apart isn't your tech stack—it's your *humanity*.

The Business Owner's Role in Brand Trust

Let's be blunt: if you're hiding behind the business name and hoping the brand will speak for itself, you're losing ground.

Your job isn't just to manage the business. It's to lead it—and to be seen leading it.

That means:

- Showing up on camera
- Speaking at events
- Posting with your name and face
- Being present in the sales process
- Owning the wins *and* the mistakes

It doesn't mean you become a full-time content creator. But it does mean your audience should feel like they know you. Because if they don't—they'll go with someone they *do* feel they know.

You've got to be in the frame—not just behind the scenes.

What It Looks Like in Practice

Let's break down how being the face of the business plays out day to day. It's not about flashy PR moves or posting daily selfies. It's about consistent, intentional visibility backed by real actions.

1. Presence in Sales When a prospect books a discovery call, make sure you show up—not just a salesperson. For example, I once joined the last ten minutes of a strategy call just to thank the prospect personally and answer one question. It closed the deal because they felt valued and heard by the person leading the business.

2. Personal Touch in Content A client of mine began sharing small video clips on LinkedIn each week—short, unpolished reflections on what she'd learned that week or how she handled a tough conversation. Her engagement tripled, and prospects began referencing her videos on discovery calls. The authenticity cut through the noise.

3. In-Person Impact Attend the networking breakfasts. Shake the hands. Be at the front of the room. At one Hashtag Event in the North West, I gave a five-minute talk. Nothing fancy. But I ended up with four new introductions and a call with a regional commercial director the next week. People buy into people they've shared space with.

4. Recognition in Community This could be as simple as sponsoring the local rugby team or being part of the same LinkedIn group every week. A fellow business owner I know became the go-to person for small business finance in her town—because she was *always* there. Not pushing, just present. Her face and name became part of the fabric of the business community.

These aren't tactics. They're habits. And when practiced consistently, they make you—and your business—impossible to ignore.

The Cost of Hiding

Let's flip it.

What happens if you *don't* show up?

- People default to your competitors—even if your offer is better.
- You miss opportunities that only happen face-to-face.
- You lose control of the narrative. If you're not telling your story, someone else will—or worse, no one will at all.
- You become another name in the noise.

Visibility is leverage. The more recognisable and trusted you are, the less resistance you face in every part of the sales and marketing process.

Building a Personal Brand That Aligns With Your Business

A personal brand isn't just a nice-to-have—it's a visibility engine. When done right, it builds equity that supports your business long after a campaign ends or a sale is made.

Here's how to build a personal brand that strengthens—not distracts from—your business:

1. Be consistent. Use the same name, photo, tone of voice, and bio across platforms. You're aiming for recognition. One of my clients, a consultant in the legal sector, used to bounce between different profile photos and taglines depending on the platform. Once we locked in a uniform look and message, she began receiving compliments on her "polished brand"—simply because she was now recognisable.

2. Stand for something. What are your values? What do you believe in? What do you say that others in your industry won't? Let people know what matters to you—this creates trust and alignment. When I started publicly calling out fluffy marketing and overcomplication in the sales world, I lost a few followers—but I gained far more respect. The people who stayed were exactly the right fit.

3. Create a recognisable rhythm. You don't need to post daily. But you do need a cadence. For example:

- Monday: A short personal insight or leadership lesson
- Wednesday: A story from the field, an event, or a client win
- Friday: A video tip, industry reflection, or recommendation

A local founder I worked with stuck to this simple pattern for three months. His visibility skyrocketed. He didn't just gain followers—he gained engagement, DMs, and meetings. Because people knew when and what to expect from him.

4. Make it personal. Show your face. Use your name. Mention your family, your background, your real experiences. Not to overshare—but to be relatable. People don't connect with perfectly curated personas. They connect with real people. I once posted about a lesson I learned from my teenage job in a pub—and it resonated more than any strategy breakdown I'd written that month.

5. Position with purpose. Use your brand to show what you do, how you think, and who you help—not just what you sell. A great example comes from a coaching client who shifted her content from "here's what I offer" to "here's how I help." Her clarity improved. Her brand improved. Her sales improved.

Your personal brand should be a lens that amplifies what makes you and your business uniquely valuable. Get this right, and your face doesn't just drive awareness—it drives trust and growth.

Real-World Example: Steven J Innes

Steven isn't just a compère or a recognisable face in golf. He's a living example of a personal brand done well. Clean, consistent visuals. A simple and memorable logo. Glasses. Groomed. Signature style.

At a recent Hashtag business networking event, I watched Steven work the room. Not by trying to sell—but by listening, remembering names, and being unmistakably himself. One business owner pulled me aside afterward and said, "I don't know what Steven does exactly, but I know I want him to host our next event." That's the power of brand association built on presence.

Steven doesn't rely on ads or gimmicks. He shows up. He's present. He's known. That's what personal branding does—it makes you memorable and referable.

And importantly—it supports his commercial brand. People book *him*, not just his service. That's the goal.

You don't have to be Steven. But you can learn from the clarity and consistency of his approach.

Owning the Narrative

One of the most overlooked parts of being the face of the business is controlling your own narrative. When you stay silent, people make assumptions. When you speak, post, and show up—you guide the perception.

Whether you're sharing your business journey, reacting to industry news, or just talking about a project you're proud of—you're shaping how people understand you. That matters.

And here's the secret: You don't need to wait until you're 'ready.'

Start now. Even if you're still figuring it out. People don't need you to be perfect—they need you to be *present*.

How to Stay Visible Without Burning Out

This isn't about turning into a social media machine or running from event to event. It's about choosing your lanes and owning them.

Here's how to stay visible without exhausting yourself:

Strategy	Example	Frequency
Pick your platform	Choose LinkedIn if you're B2B, Instagram for B2C	One-time setup
Block your visibility time	Set aside 90 minutes every Friday morning to plan and engage	Weekly
Use a simple rotation	Post Monday (insight), Wednesday (story), Friday (video)	Weekly rotation
Leverage offline time	Share a takeaway or image from a live event	As events occur
Repurpose your content	Turn client emails or talks into a weekly tip post	Ongoing

You don't need volume. You need visibility. Real, consistent, honest presence.

This isn't about turning into a social media machine or running from event to event. It's about choosing your lanes and owning them.

Here's how to stay visible without exhausting yourself:

- **Pick your platform**: Don't try to be everywhere. Choose where your audience hangs out and where you're comfortable.

- **Block your visibility time**: Just 90 minutes a week to post, follow up, and plan your presence is enough.

- **Use a simple rotation**: A post about your thoughts. A photo from an event. A video tip. Rotate, repeat.

- **Leverage your offline time**: Every event you attend gives you content. Take a picture. Share a thought. Tell a story.

- **Repurpose what you say**: Turn your emails into posts. Your talks into videos. Your conversations into blog ideas.

You don't need volume. You need visibility. Real, consistent, honest presence.

Summary: You Are the Brand

- People trust people—not companies.
- As the founder, your presence is a strategic advantage.
- Show up in your marketing, your sales, your content, and your events.
- Build a personal brand that supports your business goals.
- Be recognisable, consistent, and human.
- Use visibility to build trust faster and create inbound momentum.

You don't need to become a celebrity. You just need to become familiar.

And that means being the face of the business—because no one else can do it for you.

CHAPTER 18

You Can't Outsource Trust

We live in a world of shortcuts.

I once worked with a founder who was determined to automate everything from the start. He hired a virtual assistant overseas to handle all communications, paid for an AI to write his newsletters, and outsourced his entire marketing to a freelancer he'd never met. At first, it looked efficient. But within six months, his inbox was full of confused leads, his social content was bland and disconnected, and worst of all—he had no idea what people actually thought about his business. He had removed himself from the relationship, and with it, removed any sense of real trust.

No one knew who he was, what he stood for, or why they should care. Leads stopped converting. Referrals dried up. He hadn't built a brand—he'd built a wall between himself and the very people he was meant to serve.

Shortcuts can speed things up—but they often skip the steps that matter most. Especially the ones where trust is earned. Automated funnels. Outsourced content. AI-written blogs. Paid media. Bots handling first impressions.

But there's one thing no agency, app, or VA can do for you: **They can't build trust on your behalf.**

Trust is the currency of conversion. The asset that turns interest into commitment. And while marketing can open the door, it's trust that invites someone inside.

In this chapter, we're going deep on:

- Why trust is your job, not your agency's

- The difference between brand trust and personal trust
- What makes people *actually* trust you
- How to build it without becoming a content machine
- How trust compounds into sales, referrals, and retention

This isn't a fluffy discussion. This is about commercial impact—measurable, bankable, repeatable. Prioritising trust doesn't just make your brand feel good. It results in shorter sales cycles, fewer objections during pitches, increased customer referrals, and higher retention rates. One founder I worked with saw deal closure time drop from four weeks to ten days—simply because his clients trusted him before the first proposal landed. Another saw client lifetime value double within a year, not through upselling—but through trust and loyalty. Trust isn't abstract. It's a performance driver. Because when people trust you, they pay faster, stay longer, and refer better.

Let's dig in.

The Illusion of Delegated Credibility

Here's a truth most business owners learn too late: You can't hire someone else to be believable *for you*. I worked with a client who brought in a top-tier copywriter to run their messaging and hired a social media manager to handle engagement. The posts were polished, the responses timely, but conversions stayed flat. When we reviewed the inbound flow, we found a common thread—prospects didn't know who they were dealing with. The business felt faceless. When we replaced one weekly post with a video from the founder and included a personal note in outbound messages, response rates doubled. The trust didn't come from the polish. It came from the presence.

You can outsource design, lead gen, video editing, PR—even sales scripts. But what you can't outsource is *character*. You can't fake consistency. I've seen founders try to appear consistent by batch-scheduling months of posts, but when prospects finally reached out,

The Glue

the tone didn't match. They'd sniffed out the disconnect. True consistency means showing up in the same way, over time, and in person—not just online.

You can't buy integrity. One business I advised had a great-looking sales process, but they'd change terms mid-contract if it suited them. They lost two major clients in 30 days. Integrity is keeping your word when no one's watching. It's not for sale—and your reputation knows the difference. And you can't delegate the act of showing up.

A founder who hides behind a logo or a brand voice that never reflects a human behind it is operating at a disadvantage. Especially in a world where audiences are more suspicious, more distracted, and more flooded with empty promises than ever before.

Trust takes presence. Repetition. Exposure. Proof. In fact, if you want to reduce it to a simple but powerful idea, try this: **Trust = Presence × Consistency × Proof.** Presence gets you noticed. Consistency keeps you recognised. And proof makes your claims credible. Miss any one of those, and the whole equation breaks down. And more than anything—it takes **you**.

Brand Trust vs. Personal Trust

Let's break down something crucial.

There are two types of trust in business:

1. **Brand Trust** – Belief in the company: its products, processes, systems, guarantees.
2. **Personal Trust** – Belief in the person behind it: their integrity, values, decisions, and intentions.

You can have one without the other, but great businesses build both.

- Brand trust gets people through the door.
- Personal trust keeps them there.

- Here's an example:

Think about Virgin. People trust the company—but that trust was supercharged by Richard Branson. His personal brand added a layer of belief that the business alone could never replicate. Customers didn't just trust Virgin—they trusted *him*.

Or closer to home: I've had clients tell me, "We signed because we trust *you*—not just the service." They saw the posts, heard me speak at events, read a message that didn't feel like fluff. That built trust. The brand supported it—but the relationship sealed it.

If you think your marketing is enough to build personal trust without your face, your voice, or your presence—you're gambling. Because people trust people. Not fonts, not taglines, not templates.

You are the trust engine.

What Actually Builds Trust

We talk about trust like it's intangible, but it isn't. Trust is built on specific behaviours. You earn it with consistency and lose it with inconsistency. Here's what actually builds trust:

1. Show up consistently. People trust what they see repeatedly. If you're only visible during a launch or when you're selling, they'll associate you with noise—not value. Be the person who shows up when no one else is watching.

2. Deliver what you say you will. Follow-through builds confidence. Whether it's a proposal, a callback, or a simple promise made in a conversation—keep it. Trust compounds through small moments of integrity.

3. Be honest about limitations. People don't expect perfection. They expect clarity. Saying "that's not something we offer" or "we might not be the best fit" builds more trust than a forced yes.

4. Own your mistakes. When things go wrong, do you go silent—or do you lead? A business owner I work with recently shared a post about a project that went sideways. He didn't blame anyone. He owned it. Explained what he learned. The post had more engagement than any of his case studies. Vulnerability is credibility.

5. Be findable, not flawless. You don't need to be everywhere. But you do need to be somewhere—consistently. Whether that's on LinkedIn, in local rooms, via email—pick your channels and show up with humanity.

These aren't hacks. They're habits. And they build trust faster than any sales funnel ever could.

The Trust Timeline: It's Built in Layers

Trust doesn't come all at once—it builds in layers, and it deepens over time. One post doesn't do it. One great product doesn't lock it in. Here's how trust tends to develop in most real business relationships:

1. **Initial Signal** – A post, a recommendation, or a quick intro. You catch someone's attention with relevance, not noise.
2. **Context Building** – They start noticing your presence. A LinkedIn comment, a blog post, a short video. They realise you're not a one-off.
3. **Engagement Test** – They reach out, download something, speak to you at an event, or ask a question. This is the test—how quickly and how authentically do you respond?
4. **Proof Moment** – You deliver. You follow through. You say something that resonates. You send a useful link. This moment cements the first layer of trust.
5. **Ongoing Experience** – You continue showing up. They hear you on a podcast. See you at another event. Follow you on LinkedIn. The trust deepens into relationship.

Every layer adds weight. That's why disappearing for months or outsourcing all comms can be so damaging. People don't trust what vanishes.

You don't need to be loud. You need to be *present*. That's what builds lasting, commercial trust.

Trust in Sales vs. Trust in Marketing

Marketing opens the door, but sales builds the relationship.

Too often, businesses confuse visibility with credibility. Just because someone sees your ad or lands on your homepage doesn't mean they trust you. Marketing can start the journey, but without trust embedded into your sales process, the conversion never happens.

What builds trust in marketing?

- Real photos, not stock.
- Clear messaging, not fluff.
- Social proof: reviews, case studies, testimonials.
- Transparency around pricing, expectations, and outcomes.

What builds trust in sales?

- Listening more than speaking.
- Asking thoughtful, non-scripted questions.
- Repeating back what you heard to prove you understand.
- Following up when you said you would.

Trust in sales is about moments. The pause before answering a tough question. The honesty about what's not included. The speed of the proposal. The tone of the follow-up.

I've had clients say, "It wasn't your pitch—it was how you handled the question about timeframes." That's trust being formed in real time.

When sales and marketing both carry trust forward, your conversions rise and your churn drops.

Where Agencies Go Wrong (And How to Fix It)

Let's talk honestly about agencies. There are brilliant ones out there. I work alongside some. But there's a common problem in how most business owners use them:

They outsource too much of the relationship.

You hire someone to run your LinkedIn. To write your blog. To follow up leads. And before long, your voice has disappeared. The tone is off. The content sounds like everyone else. And your audience knows it.

Here's where agencies go wrong:

- They prioritise volume over value.
- They chase reach, not resonance.
- They speak *for* you, instead of *with* you.

The result? Generic output. A brand that sounds like it was built by committee. A pipeline filled with cold leads who don't know who you are.

How to fix it:

- Don't abdicate—collaborate. You stay the face. They help with the framework.
- Feed them stories, voice notes, personal takes.
- Review everything through the lens of trust: Does this feel real? Does it sound like me?

A great agency should enhance your presence, not replace it. They can build reach—but you build *relationship*.

Trust can be supported externally, but it must be *anchored* in you.

The Compounding Power of Trust

Trust isn't just about today's sale. It's the multiplier on all your future efforts. When people trust you:

- Your emails get opened.
- Your posts get shared.
- Your quotes get accepted.
- Your clients become ambassadors.

I've worked with founders who built small but fiercely loyal client bases—just by showing up honestly. One in particular didn't have a fancy website, a slick deck, or a strong ad strategy. But what he did have was reputation. People said, "You can count on him."

That kind of trust doesn't just generate sales. It shortens sales cycles. It softens objections. It creates loyalty in industries where clients usually churn fast.

And the best part? Trust scales.

One happy client becomes three referrals. One post that lands well creates months of inbound interest. One podcast appearance turns into a keynote because someone liked how honest you were.

The return on trust is exponential.

That's why this chapter matters. That's why being visible, present, and consistent *matters*.

Final Word: Make Trust the Strategy

Most business owners obsess over tactics—funnels, outreach, algorithms, systems.

But the strategy that never fails is trust.

Trust isn't soft. It's commercial. It's not a luxury. It's a multiplier. It's not a side effect. It's the goal.

If you want:

- Better leads
- Faster sales
- Fewer objections
- More referrals
- Higher retention

…then build trust.

You build it by showing up. You build it by speaking like a human. You build it by owning your voice, not outsourcing your identity.

And when you do—your business stops needing to shout. Because your clients do the talking for you.

That's the power of trust.

You can't outsource it. But when you own it, everything else becomes easier.

Make trust your competitive edge. Because when people trust *you*—everything works better.

PART 5

Impact & Implementation

CHAPTER 19

The Glue in Action

If this book had a heartbeat, this chapter would be it.

You've seen the philosophy. You've explored the mindset. You've worked through the structure. Now it's time to bring it all together—the glue that binds sales and marketing in a real, working business.

This isn't theory. This is application.

We're going to break down:

- What alignment looks like when it's working
- Where most teams break down and why
- How to rebuild a joined-up commercial engine
- The playbook you can implement immediately

Sales and marketing aren't just departments. They're two ends of the same system. When they pull together, momentum builds. When they pull apart, everything stalls.

Alignment isn't about fluffy values or cross-department meetings with biscuits. It's about shared focus, shared accountability, and shared outcomes.

This chapter will show you how to make that happen.

Let's put the glue into action.

What Alignment Really Looks Like

Let's start with the good stuff—what does it actually look like when sales and marketing are aligned?

It's not a perfect spreadsheet or colour-coded campaign calendar. It's this:

- Sales are having better conversations because leads are warmed up and informed.

- Marketing is creating content based on actual sales objections, not guesses.

- Everyone's working to the same revenue target—not vanity metrics.

- Weekly feedback loops exist. Sales tells marketing what's working. Marketing tells sales what's resonating.

- There's one clear pipeline with clear definitions: lead, prospect, opportunity, close.

- Everyone knows the customer journey—because they built it together.

Let me give you a real-world example. One client, a specialist recruitment firm, struggled for years with inconsistent results. Marketing were producing tons of content—blogs, emails, social posts—but sales weren't using any of it. The teams sat in different rooms, answered to different KPIs, and rarely spoke.

Once we aligned them, everything shifted. Sales and marketing agreed on the same pipeline stages. They set shared weekly targets around conversations booked, not content created. Marketing began writing based on sales scripts and objections. Within 90 days, conversion rates jumped by 28% and close time reduced by a full week.

Another client, a regional IT company, had great awareness but terrible follow-through. Marketing was winning awards for their brand campaigns, but sales couldn't close because leads were cold and confused. We rebuilt their journey from the ground up—with joint messaging, clearer targeting, and co-owned nurturing sequences. In six months, client satisfaction rose, churn dropped by 40%, and inbound referrals doubled.

In aligned businesses, the commercial engine feels smooth. Not frictionless—real growth always includes bumps—but there's shared direction. And shared responsibility.

You don't hear "That's a sales problem" or "Marketing didn't give us good leads." You hear: "Let's figure it out together."

Where the Breakdown Happens

Most businesses don't lack talent. They lack unity.

Here's where things usually fall apart:

1. Different definitions of success. Sales wants signed contracts. Marketing celebrates clicks and downloads. No shared language. No shared scoreboard.

2. No feedback loop. Sales doesn't tell marketing what prospects are asking. Marketing doesn't ask sales what they need. Everyone guesses—and misses.

3. Silos and egos. Sales thinks marketing sits in a room writing fluffy taglines. Marketing thinks salespeople wing it on every call. Both underestimate the other.

4. Broken handovers. Marketing hands off leads with no context. Sales doesn't follow up quickly—or worse, not at all. Leads get cold. Everyone blames everyone.

5. No commercial leadership. There's no one pulling the two functions together. No glue. No alignment. No accountability.

Here's a real example. One business I worked with had strong individual teams—marketing were producing high-quality thought leadership content, and sales were experienced closers. But they operated in silos. Marketing was generating leads that were technically relevant, but completely unqualified. Sales followed up only to find the lead had no budget, no authority, or no urgency. The result? Poor conversion, internal frustration, and wasted budget.

After three months of this, the managing director had to intervene. We discovered that marketing were using outdated personas and targeting the wrong segment entirely. Meanwhile, sales had a goldmine of insight about who the best clients were—but no channel to feed it back. The misalignment had real cost: three months of pipeline with no ROI.

Sound familiar?

It doesn't have to be this way.

You can fix it—and you can do it with what you already have.

How to Rebuild the Glue

Now let's fix it—step by step. This is how you re-glue your sales and marketing into one system, not two functions.

Step 1: Build a Shared Language

Create clear definitions for:

- What is a lead?
- What makes it qualified?
- When does marketing hand off?
- When is sales responsible?

Put it in writing. Make it simple. This language becomes your commercial blueprint.

One business I supported had a marketing team referring to 'leads' as anyone who downloaded a PDF, while sales only considered someone a lead if they'd requested a quote. The disconnect was enormous. Once they created a shared language and agreed on three qualification stages, both teams began working off the same page—

literally. Pipeline reports became more meaningful, and follow-up improved immediately.

Step 2: Align on the Real Goal

If your marketing team is chasing impressions while your sales team is chasing signed contracts, you're not aligned. Set a joint commercial goal. Usually: revenue. Then build activity KPIs that contribute to that goal for both teams.

At a SaaS company I advised, the marketing team celebrated a huge spike in webinar attendees—but none of them were qualified. Sales were left holding the bag. When we redefined success around demo bookings instead of attendees, both teams changed their behaviour. Campaigns became tighter. Messaging improved. Conversion increased by 22% the following quarter.

Step 3: Design the Feedback Loop

Every week—yes, every week—sales and marketing should talk. Here's a simple agenda:

- What content worked?
- What objections did we hear?
- What questions came up?
- What deals closed and why?
- What leads went cold and when?

You're not just collecting info. You're shaping strategy together.

One of the most effective versions I've seen was a standing Friday 15-minute Zoom call where one rep from sales and one from marketing shared wins, losses, and one new insight. It wasn't fancy—but it forced dialogue. Within a month, the tone of content had changed, and engagement improved.

Step 4: Fix the Handover

Build a clear lead handover system:

- CRM tags
- Lead notes
- Source details
- First step suggestions

Marketing doesn't just throw leads over the fence. Sales doesn't just "pick it up from there." The baton is passed—with context.

A digital agency I worked with reduced lead drop-off by 35% in one quarter by introducing a structured lead handover form. It included where the lead came from, what they'd downloaded, and what their last action was. Sales could open the CRM and pick up the conversation naturally. Leads felt seen—not sold to.

Step 5: Create Shared Assets

This is where the magic happens.

- Marketing writes the email templates—but sales feeds the language.
- Sales creates voice notes—but marketing turns them into posts.
- Marketing builds a guide—but sales helps shape the headline.

I've watched businesses cut content production time in half simply by tapping into recorded sales calls. Sales provided raw voice notes, marketing cleaned it up and distributed it—everyone won.

Step 6: Appoint a Commercial Leader

Call them a Commercial Director, a Revenue Manager, or the Glue. But someone has to own the full journey. This person's job? Keep the engine aligned. Track the numbers. Remove friction. Protect the focus.

In one consultancy, we appointed a Commercial Lead—not a senior hire, but someone mid-level with credibility on both teams. They ran fortnightly huddles, owned the pipeline board, and acted as referee when alignment drifted. Revenue consistency improved in 60 days.

When you rebuild the glue this way, you're not just fixing a broken system. You're creating a new one that works better than anything siloed ever could.

The Glue Playbook (Real Business Edition)

Here's what I use with clients to join it all up:

Quarterly Planning:

- Revenue targets set with sales and marketing in the room.
- Campaign themes agreed by both sides.
- Tools audited. Roles clarified.

Monthly Commercial Reviews:

- Performance check-in on joint KPIs.
- Pipeline review and lead source analysis.
- Objection and message analysis.

Weekly Stand-ups (30 mins max):

- Key activity wins and gaps.
- Priority content/assets needed.
- Campaign status and lead quality.

Shared Tools:

- One CRM used by all.
- Shared Slack/WhatsApp for quick comms.
- Scoreboard dashboard tracking activity > pipeline > revenue.

Simple. Repeatable. Effective.

What Happens When It's Working

When the glue sets, everything changes:

- Sales starts each week knowing exactly where to focus.
- Marketing finally hears, in real time, how content is landing.
- Clients experience a consistent tone and journey from first touch to long-term relationship.
- Your commercial strategy stops relying on the founder showing up everywhere—and becomes scalable.

Let me show you what this looks like in real life.

One of my clients, a software development firm, was stuck in a loop of stalled deals and inconsistent messaging. Sales would make bold claims in pitches that didn't match the marketing material. Marketing was pushing top-of-funnel blogs with no input from the sales floor. Clients were confused. The trust gap widened. Revenue flatlined.

We stepped in and created a unified content calendar, built weekly feedback calls, and established a single sales-marketing Slack channel. Sales started feeding live objections into content planning. Marketing began producing decision-stage assets designed for one-on-one conversations. The founder pulled back from micromanaging and started enabling the team.

Within six months, they doubled their conversion rate on inbound leads. Sales cycles shortened by 40%. And perhaps most importantly—the business finally felt aligned from the inside out.

When sales and marketing work as one:

- You win faster.
- You retain longer.
- You build something worth scaling.

- When the glue sets, everything changes:
- Sales starts each week knowing exactly where to focus.
- Marketing finally hears, in real time, how content is landing.
- Clients experience a consistent tone and journey from first touch to long-term relationship.
- Your commercial strategy stops relying on the founder showing up everywhere—and becomes scalable.

I've watched businesses triple their revenue in under 18 months—not because they spent more, but because they aligned more. They stopped running parallel functions and started operating one machine. And that's the difference.

Final Word: Glue Is a Leadership Job

If you're the founder, director, or commercial lead—this chapter is your mirror.

Alignment doesn't happen in a workshop. It happens when someone decides to lead it.

The glue between sales and marketing isn't a software. It's a mindset. It's the daily decision to work as one team with one goal, driven by real feedback and shared ownership.

No one is coming to do this for you. You have to choose to be the glue.

Because when you are—it sticks. And when it sticks, the whole machine moves together.

That's what this book has been about. And now, you've got everything you need to make it happen.

CHAPTER 20

The 6-Month Growth Plan

If you've made it this far, you're not just a reader—you're a builder.

You've worked your way through strategy, structure, leadership, alignment, visibility, and trust. You understand why sales and marketing must stick together. You know the common pitfalls, and you've seen the roadmap laid out.

Now it's time to act.

This chapter is your tactical plan—designed to be implemented over six months. Not six years. Not some lofty transformation vision that never happens. This is real, gritty, focused growth.

The plan is simple. One key focus per month. Each builds on the last. And by the end of it, you'll have a joined-up commercial engine—not just two teams doing different things.

We're not just making more noise. We're building something that converts.

Month 1: Map the Mess

Before you can fix anything, you need to see it.

Your focus this month: **Diagnosis**.

Goals:

- Understand your full sales and marketing ecosystem
- Identify bottlenecks, silos, and gaps
- Establish a baseline for leads, conversions, and follow-up

Tasks:

1. Map your entire lead flow—from awareness to close.
2. List every tool you use (CRM, email, automation, outreach, content creation, social, etc).
3. Review the last 10 leads: where they came from, what happened, what didn't.
4. Interview your team. Ask:
    a. Where do most leads come from?
    b. What's the handover process?
    c. What objections do we hear repeatedly?
    d. Where do leads fall through the cracks?
5. Hold one joint meeting between sales and marketing to share insights.

Case Example:

One business we worked with, a B2B service provider, thought their pipeline was solid. Leads were coming in, meetings were booked—but sales kept missing targets. In Month 1, we helped them map every stage of their lead flow.

The outcome? They discovered that 43% of leads dropped off completely after the initial discovery call. Why? There was no follow-up system. No accountability. No automation. This insight led them to rework their CRM process and create templated follow-ups. The very next quarter, conversions increased by 19%.

Another client—an e-commerce brand—believed their marketing was underperforming. But mapping the mess showed the issue was at the top of the funnel. Website visitors were clicking "contact us" but no one was assigned to follow up. The gap? Ownership. Once assigned, lead response time dropped from 72 hours to 3. Sales jumped 26% in two months.

Deliverable:

A one-page map of your sales-marketing journey with friction points clearly marked.

Before you can fix anything, you need to see it.

Your focus this month: **Diagnosis**.

Goals:

- Understand your full sales and marketing ecosystem
- Identify bottlenecks, silos, and gaps
- Establish a baseline for leads, conversions, and follow-up

Tasks:

1. Map your entire lead flow—from awareness to close.
2. List every tool you use (CRM, email, automation, outreach, content creation, social, etc).
3. Review the last 10 leads: where they came from, what happened, what didn't.
4. Interview your team. Ask:
    a. Where do most leads come from?
    b. What's the handover process?
    c. What objections do we hear repeatedly?
    d. Where do leads fall through the cracks?
5. Hold one joint meeting between sales and marketing to share insights.

Deliverable:

A one-page map of your sales-marketing journey with friction points clearly marked.

Month 2: Rebuild the Foundation

Now that you've found the friction, it's time to reset the rules.

Your focus this month: **Alignment**.

Goals:

- Build shared definitions for leads,
- Re-align sales and marketing toward one commercial goal

Tasks:

1. Define what makes a lead qualified. Write it down.
2. Redefine pipeline stages with shared language across both teams.
3. Set a joint commercial target (e.g. revenue, demos booked, proposal value).
4. Audit and simplify tools—merge where possible.
5. Launch weekly 30-minute sales-marketing syncs.

Deliverable:

A Commercial Alignment Document—covering definitions, targets, pipeline stages, and sync schedules.

Month 3: Build the Follow-Up Engine

This month is where most small businesses create their biggest wins.

Your focus this month: **Conversion & Follow-Up**.

Goals:

- Fix follow-up gaps
- Standardise key messaging
- Reduce lead response time

Tasks:

1. Build a lead tracker with lead stage, source, owner, and next step.
2. Write follow-up templates for:
    a. Initial reply
    b. No-response nudge
    c. Objection response
    d. Final check-in
2. Introduce a simple system for lead scoring (Hot / Warm / Cold).
3. Set internal SLAs (e.g. every lead gets a response within 1 business day).
4. Add 1–2 lead nurture emails based on interest or download history.

Deliverable:

A repeatable follow-up workflow built into your CRM or spreadsheet.

Month 4: Create with Purpose

Time to stop guessing what to post and start building content that converts.

Your focus this month: **Strategic Content**.

Goals:

- Produce content tied to the sales journey
- Create repurposable assets from real conversations

Tasks:

1. Interview 3–5 clients or prospects. Ask:

a. What made you choose us?

   b. What nearly stopped you?

   c. What would you tell someone considering us?

2. Write 3 sales emails and 3 marketing posts based on the answers.

3. Repurpose sales call insights into:

   a. A social post

   b. A blog

   c. A short video

4. Align content topics with pipeline stages (awareness, interest, action).

5. Collaborate: Sales feeds raw notes. Marketing turns them into assets.

Deliverable:

A shared content bank aligned with objections, stages, and lead types.

Month 5: Activate Outbound

You've built a strong inbound system. Now it's time to go hunting.

Your focus this month: **Outbound Prospecting**.

Goals:

- Test and scale a simple outbound flow

- Combine personalisation with automation

Tasks:

1. Define your outbound audience (ideal client profile + buying signals).

2. Create a 3-message sequence:
   a. Connection + value
   b. Question / hook
   c. CTA (call, download, audit, etc.)
3. Test via email, LinkedIn, or other relevant channels.
4. Log results weekly: opens, replies, meetings.
5. Optimise based on what converts—not what feels safe.

Deliverable:

An outbound sequence in place, tested, and improving.

Month 6: Scale the System

You've got the foundation. Now it's time to make it repeatable.

Your focus this month: **Consistency & Leadership**.

Goals:

- Systematise what's working
- Delegate without losing quality
- Build leadership into the process

Tasks:

1. Review the last 5 months. What's working? What's not?
2. Assign ownership for each stage (who runs what, when).
3. Automate the basics:
   a. New lead alerts
   b. Calendar links
   c. Lead source tagging
   d. Reporting dashboards
4. Create a Monthly Commercial Review template.

5 Document your full sales-marketing system in a living playbook.

Deliverable:

A repeatable growth system—with people, process, and metrics defined.

Bonus: Your Commercial Leadership Checklist

Whether you're a founder, director, or sales lead, this checklist keeps the glue in place:

Weekly:

- Join or run a 30-minute sales-marketing sync
- Review pipeline movements
- Track lead source performance

Monthly:

- Review content effectiveness
- Adjust lead scoring based on outcomes
- Recalibrate outbound targeting

Quarterly:

- Set/confirm revenue goals
- Audit tools and eliminate clutter
- Update your Commercial Playbook

Always:

- Ask your team: "What's missing from our glue right now?"
- Protect momentum.
- Lead visibly.

CHAPTER 21

The Glue in Practice: 20 Quick Wins to Create Sales & Marketing Alignment

You've got the philosophy. You've got the plan. Now it's time to execute.

This chapter is your *Quick Wins* playbook. It's not fluff. It's not theory. These are real, tactical actions you can implement within the next 30 days to build momentum, unify your teams, and start closing the gap between sales and marketing—fast.

If the main chapters of this book gave you the strategy, this is the starter's gun.

Here are 20 practical alignment wins to embed the glue into your business from day one.

1. Schedule a Sales-Marketing Alignment Meeting This Week

Purpose: Start the conversation. **Impact:** Creates immediate visibility and collaboration. **Action:** Book a 45-minute session where both teams share current priorities, campaign ideas, and what's working/not working.

2. Define One Shared Commercial Goal

Purpose: Unify direction. **Impact:** Gets everyone pulling in the same direction. **Action:** Choose a single, commercial target (e.g. revenue, number of new clients) for both teams to focus on this quarter.

3. Build a Shared Language Document

Purpose: Align messaging. **Impact:** Eliminates mixed messages and confusion. **Action:** Create a shared doc with your key brand phrases, pain points, value statements, and offer headlines. Keep it live.

4. Review 5 Recent Sales Calls Together

Purpose: Transfer frontline insight into campaigns. **Impact:** Improves relevance and targeting. **Action:** Pick 5 recent sales calls, listen together, and extract key objections, phrases, and stories that could feed your next campaign.

5. Identify the Top 3 Sales Objections—and Create Content Around Them

Purpose: Equip marketing to support conversion. **Impact:** Strengthens buyer confidence. **Action:** Use FAQs, social posts, videos, and landing pages to proactively address objections.

6. Create a Campaign Performance Scorecard

Purpose: Track outcomes, not just outputs. **Impact:** Builds data-led accountability. **Action:** Set up a monthly scoreboard with inputs (leads, reach) and outcomes (conversions, revenue). Review with both teams.

7. Run a "Voice of the Customer" Review

Purpose: Refocus messaging on real-world language. **Impact:** Boosts resonance and results. **Action:** Collect and review testimonials, reviews, and email replies. Identify exact phrases and emotions your buyers use.

8. Host a 90-Minute Alignment Workshop

Purpose: Set a cultural tone. **Impact:** Breaks silos and builds energy. **Action:** Bring everyone together. Walk through your funnel. Clarify handovers. Align on brand voice. Share the strategy.

9. Align on Lead Qualification Criteria

Purpose: Avoid chasing the wrong leads. **Impact:** Improves close rates and sales efficiency. **Action:** Define what qualifies a lead as "sales-ready." Use that criteria to score inbound leads.

10. Build a Real-Time Feedback Loop

Purpose: Close the communication gap. **Impact:** Makes improvement continuous. **Action:** Create a simple Slack channel, WhatsApp group, or weekly form where sales can give quick feedback on leads and messaging.

11. Create a Single Sales + Marketing Calendar

Purpose: Unite planning. **Impact:** Prevents last-minute chaos. **Action:** Merge campaign dates, product launches, holidays, and key events. One calendar = one rhythm.

12. Make the Founder Visible in Campaigns

Purpose: Build trust and credibility. **Impact:** Increases engagement and conversion. **Action:** Film a short founder message, do a behind-the-scenes post, or run a Q&A session on LinkedIn or email.

13. Introduce Weekly Alignment Reviews

Purpose: Keep momentum consistent. **Impact:** Solves issues early. **Action:** Spend 15 minutes every Monday checking alignment: priorities, problems, and performance. Fast feedback = fast fixes.

14. Repurpose Sales Wins as Social Proof

Purpose: Turn conversions into content. **Impact:** Increases credibility and relatability. **Action:** Document every sale, case study, or positive client message. Use these in marketing emails, social posts, and sales decks.

15. Map Content to the Buyer Journey

The Glue

Purpose: Serve the right message at the right time. **Impact:** Reduces drop-off and increases flow. **Action:** Audit current content. Tag each item: Awareness, Consideration, or Decision stage. Fill the gaps with relevant content.

16. Train Sales on the Marketing Message

Purpose: Ensure consistency in pitch. **Impact:** Builds buyer confidence. **Action:** Walk through your website, ads, and key assets with the sales team. Align tone, phrases, and positioning.

17. Capture and Share a Real Client Story

Purpose: Show—not just tell. **Impact:** Builds trust through narrative. **Action:** Interview a happy client. Turn it into a short video, blog, or email story. Share it across platforms.

18. Agree on Campaign Success Criteria

Purpose: Avoid post-launch confusion. **Impact:** Clarifies expectations. **Action:** For every campaign, agree in advance: What does success look like? Leads? Sales? Awareness? Define it. Track it.

19. Remove One Siloed Tool or Process

Purpose: Simplify and unify. **Impact:** Boosts operational flow. **Action:** Audit your current sales/marketing stack. Identify one tool that's redundant, confusing, or underused. Cut it or consolidate.

20. Celebrate a Shared Win Publicly

Purpose: Reinforce the right culture. **Impact:** Builds belief and morale. **Action:** When a campaign or sales surge works, celebrate it. Tag both teams. Call out collaboration. Culture grows where energy flows.

Bringing It All Together

These 20 wins aren't one-offs—they're habits. You don't have to do them all at once. But if you do even five this month, your sales and marketing function will look and feel different.

The glue isn't just about what you believe—it's about what you build. And these actions build culture, momentum, and results.

Print this page. Share it with your team. Make it part of your monthly rhythm.

Because aligned businesses aren't just smarter. They're faster, stronger, and built to last.

This is the glue—in practice.

CHAPTER 22

Common Mistakes That Kill Sales & Marketing Alignment

This section is not here to criticise—it's here to clarify. Because when alignment fails, it's rarely due to bad intent. More often, it's due to blind spots, assumptions, and avoidable errors.

Over the years, I've seen the same mistakes repeat themselves across industries, budgets, and business sizes. From solo founders to multi-location teams, these patterns show up again and again.

If you want to maintain the momentum this book has built, it's just as important to avoid these common traps as it is to follow best practices. Consider this your "anti-checklist."

Let's get into the real-world errors that quietly sabotage growth.

1. Treating Sales and Marketing as Separate Entities

The Mistake: Organising your business like sales and marketing are different sports, played on different pitches.

What it looks like:

- Separate meetings, separate dashboards, separate language.
- Sales complaining about lead quality. Marketing complaining about follow-up.
- "That's not my job" creeping into the culture.

The Fix: Create joint objectives. One shared commercial goal. One campaign calendar. One review rhythm. Sales and marketing should co-own the outcome.

2. Prioritising Vanity Metrics Over Real Results

The Mistake: Confusing activity for progress. Elevating impressions, likes, or traffic over leads, conversions, and revenue.

What it looks like:

- Celebrating engagement while revenue drops.
- Weekly reports that never mention sales outcomes.
- Marketing judged by volume, not value.

The Fix: Reset your metrics. If a KPI doesn't impact commercial performance, it's not a KPI—it's noise.

3. Failing to Involve Sales in Campaign Planning

The Mistake: Building marketing campaigns in a vacuum.

What it looks like:

- Launching a campaign that targets the wrong pain point.
- Creative ideas that don't support the actual sales conversation.
- A sales team caught off guard by "the new offer."

The Fix: Involve sales in campaign ideation. Review drafts together. Base campaigns on sales insights, not creative inspiration.

4. No Feedback Loop Between Teams

The Mistake: Allowing months to go by without structured review.

What it looks like:

- Sales learn things from prospects—but marketing never hears it.
- Marketing gets performance data—but doesn't share it with sales.
- Lessons are lost. Wins aren't repeated.

The Fix: Weekly feedback loops. A 15-minute debrief on what's working and what's not. Formalise it. Don't leave it to chance.

5. Over-Reliance on Automation

The Mistake: Thinking a CRM or automation tool will fix a broken process.

What it looks like:

- Over-complicated workflows no one understands.
- Automated messages that feel cold or irrelevant.
- Leads slipping through the cracks because no human is watching.

The Fix: Automation should support alignment, not replace it. Start with a simple manual process that works—then automate from there.

6. Lack of Commercial Leadership

The Mistake: No one owns the outcome.

What it looks like:

- Marketing managers focused on content. Sales managers focused on closing. Nobody focused on how it all connects.
- Confusion about priorities.
- Strategy drifting instead of driving.

The Fix: Assign commercial leadership. Whether it's a fractional director or internal lead, someone has to own the full growth picture.

7. Reactive Rather Than Proactive Planning

The Mistake: Jumping from campaign to campaign without a long-term plan.

What it looks like:

- Endless short-term pushes with no lasting impact.

- Sales team overwhelmed with changing priorities.
- Marketing constantly behind, chasing deadlines.

The Fix: Build a quarterly rhythm. Plan campaigns 30–60 days in advance. Give both teams time to prepare and optimise.

8. No Sales Training on the Marketing Message

The Mistake: Assuming the sales team understands the offer just because it was written in a brochure.

What it looks like:

- Sales calls that contradict your website.
- Misalignment on what makes your offer valuable.
- Mixed messages creating doubt for the buyer.

The Fix: Train the sales team on the marketing message. Role-play the pitch. Use the same language across all channels.

9. Ignoring the Buyer Journey

The Mistake: Sending the same message to everyone, regardless of where they are in the funnel.

What it looks like:

- Cold leads getting closing offers.
- Warm leads not getting nurtured.
- Marketing sending traffic, but not context.

The Fix: Map the buyer journey. Align campaigns and content to each stage. Match message to mindset.

10. Not Using Real Results in Marketing

The Mistake: Overlooking the most persuasive asset you have—proof.

What it looks like:

- Social posts without substance.
- Websites full of buzzwords, empty of evidence.
- Sales left to convince prospects without support.

The Fix: Document success stories. Share results. Turn wins into content. Make credibility part of the campaign.

11. No Defined Lead Qualification Criteria

The Mistake: Letting marketing and sales work off different definitions of a "good lead."

What it looks like:

- Sales chasing unqualified enquiries.
- Marketing generating volume, not value.
- Frustration and finger-pointing.

The Fix: Create a shared lead scoring system. Define ideal client criteria. Review monthly.

12. Underestimating the Importance of Offline Presence

The Mistake: Believing everything important happens online.

What it looks like:

- No one attending industry events or networking.
- Relationships limited to DMs and email.
- Visibility only exists in pixels, not in people's minds.

The Fix: Mix digital and real-world activity. Get visible in rooms. Meet people. Offline trust leads to online traction.

13. Content Without Context

The Mistake: Posting content for content's sake.

What it looks like:

- Generic advice that could apply to any business.
- High volume, low relevance.
- Engagement without conversion.

The Fix: Root every piece of content in a real conversation, insight, or customer need. Start with context, then create.

14. Trying to Outsource the Message Too Soon

The Mistake: Handing off brand communication to a third party before it's fully formed.

What it looks like:

- Agencies writing copy that doesn't sound like you.
- Campaigns that feel off-brand or disconnected.
- Wasted time, money, and momentum.

The Fix: Own the message first. Nail your story, tone, and value. Only then bring in external support.

15. Lack of Consistency in Review & Optimisation

The Mistake: Set and forget marketing. "We ran the campaign, now we move on."

What it looks like:

- No debrief after launches.
- Wins and losses not documented.
- Teams making the same mistakes repeatedly.

The Fix: Build in monthly reviews. Celebrate what worked. Kill what didn't. Optimise the next round.

Wrap-Up: Mistakes Don't Have to Be Fatal

Most businesses don't fail because of one big decision—they fade because of a thousand small misalignments.

This list is your prevention tool. Come back to it quarterly. Use it in your leadership reviews. Ask your team: *Which of these are we making right now? What would it look like to fix it this month?*

You don't have to be perfect to win. But you do have to be aware.

Awareness creates alignment.

Alignment creates momentum.

And momentum—sustained over time—is what builds real, long-term growth.

Avoid these mistakes, and you're already ahead of 90% of your competitors.

Let's keep moving forward—on purpose, together.

CHAPTER 23

Checklist Summary: Real-World Alignment in Action

If you've reached this point in the book, you understand something most business owners never do:

Sales and marketing are not separate—they are two sides of the same growth engine. Alignment isn't just about communication. It's about shared purpose, shared accountability, and shared results.

This checklist isn't a formality. It's your new operational baseline. It's a practical, tactical review guide to keep you focused on real alignment—week by week, quarter by quarter. Think of it as your internal audit.

Use it with your team. Use it solo. But use it. This is where clarity becomes consistency—and consistency becomes growth.

1. COMMERCIAL ALIGNMENT

Alignment starts at the top. If your leadership isn't commercially aligned, everything below it fractures.

- Do we have a clearly defined commercial goal this quarter?
- Is our sales target aligned with our delivery capacity?
- Does the marketing team know what the sales team needs this month?
- Are we prioritising profit-generating activity over brand-building fluff?

Red flag: If marketing can't explain what sales needs this week, you're misaligned.

2. SHARED LANGUAGE & MESSAGING

Confusion kills conversion. If sales and marketing are using different language, the customer feels it.

- **Are we using the same pain points and phrases across sales decks, ads, and web copy?**
- **Are we consistent in how we describe our product or service?**
- **Are we explaining value from the buyer's perspective—not our own?**
- **Has the sales team signed off on the core marketing message?**

Quick win: Hold a 30-minute alignment workshop. Compare ad copy, sales decks, and landing pages. Highlight inconsistencies. Fix them.

3. PIPELINE PRECISION

Your pipeline isn't a funnel—it's a flow. And marketing's job is to feed it with quality, not just quantity.

- **Do we have visibility on every stage of the sales pipeline?**
- **Are leads tracked and categorised (cold, warm, hot) with clarity?**
- **Are marketing campaigns focused on generating qualified leads—not vanity metrics?**
- **Does the sales team report back on lead quality weekly?**
- **Is there a documented feedback loop from sales to marketing?**

Best practice: Create a weekly report that scores lead quality by campaign. Use it to double down on what's working and kill what's not.

4. CONTENT & CAMPAIGN CADENCE

Good campaigns are not about creativity—they're about consistency.

- Do we have a structured content plan that maps to each stage of the buyer journey?
- Are we reviewing campaign performance monthly, with both sales and marketing present?
- Are we telling real stories (case studies, testimonials, behind-the-scenes)—not just posting content for the sake of it?
- Are we repurposing sales call insights into marketing content?
- Do we have a clear rhythm (weekly/monthly) for publishing, promoting, and reviewing content?

Tip: Your best campaign ideas are already in your business. Talk to the team. Talk to customers. Mine your inbox.

5. LEAD HANDOVER & FOLLOW-UP

Most leads don't fall through because of a lack of interest—they fall through because of a lack of process.

- Is there a crystal-clear handover point between marketing and sales?
- Are leads followed up within 24 hours, every time?
- Are follow-up templates and scripts created with marketing input?
- Are leads tracked from first click to closed deal?

- Is someone accountable for following up on every lead—not just "checking in" but advancing the sale?

Note: Follow-up is the most overlooked growth activity in the business. It's also the cheapest to fix.

6. DATA-DRIVEN DECISIONS

Feelings don't build businesses. Data does.

- Do we have one source of truth for marketing and sales metrics?
- Are we measuring conversion rates, not just clicks or impressions?
- Are KPIs tied to outcomes (leads closed, revenue generated) rather than outputs (posts made, ads run)?
- Are decisions made based on data—not politics, preferences, or guesswork?
- Are we reviewing performance monthly and adjusting accordingly?

Danger zone: If data isn't influencing your next campaign, you're flying blind.

7. TEAM STRUCTURE & COMMUNICATION

Alignment is a leadership function. It has to be modelled, not mandated.

- Are sales and marketing part of the same leadership conversations?
- Do we have regular joint meetings (weekly or biweekly) to review pipeline and campaign progress?
- Are we rewarding cross-functional wins—not just silo performance?

- Is someone accountable for sales and marketing working together?

- Does our team know who owns what—and who to talk to when?

Fix it fast: One owner. One point of contact. One shared result. Don't let things fall between the cracks.

8. FOUNDER VISIBILITY & LEADERSHIP

If you're reading this book, you're not just the founder—you're the glue.

- Are you visibly supporting both teams—internally and externally?

- Are you reinforcing the company's mission and messaging regularly?

- Are you showing up as the face of the brand online and in person?

- Are you leading with commercial focus, not just creative energy?

- Are you protecting time for high-value sales and marketing leadership—not just operations?

Reminder: Culture follows visibility. If your team doesn't see you prioritising alignment, they won't either.

Final Notes

This checklist is a reflection tool—not a pass/fail test. Use it weekly. Use it with your team. Share it at your next offsite.

It's not about perfection. It's about progress.

The more you align, the more you grow. The more you review, the more you improve. The more you show up, the more your team will too.

Print this page. Mark it up. Revisit it every 30 days. Ask: *Where are we strong? Where are we slipping? What's the one change we can make this month to close the gap?*

Alignment doesn't happen by accident. But with this structure, it does happen by design.

That's the glue in practice.

CHAPTER 24

About Momentum – Sales & Marketing, Aligned for Growth

This book wasn't written to impress. It was written to help.

And if you've reached this point, you now understand the full picture: when sales and marketing operate in silos, your business stalls. But when they align, you gain traction, visibility, and sustainable growth.

Now the question becomes—how do you make it stick?

How do you turn this philosophy into practice? How do you bridge the gap between knowing what to do and actually doing it consistently?

That's why I created Momentum.

This chapter is not a sales pitch. It's a look behind the curtain at what Momentum does, how we do it, and why it might be the missing piece in your business if you're serious about implementing what you've just read.

Why Momentum Exists

Momentum Sales & Marketing was born out of frustration. Not just mine—but the frustration of business owners who had:

- Tried agencies, but never saw a commercial return.
- Hired internal teams, but lacked clear direction.
- Invested in marketing, only to see leads stall or vanish.
- Trusted salespeople who couldn't convert.

I've been there. I've owned multiple businesses. I've made the marketing mistakes. I've pushed the wrong sales tactics. I've spent money on the wrong tools. And I've learned—usually the hard way—that no growth strategy works unless sales and marketing work *together*.

Momentum is the business I wish I had alongside me in the early days: a trusted, agile team that *gets* commercial reality and has the capability to build and implement everything from strategy to campaigns to CRM and lead flow.

We don't theorise. We don't just advise. We build with you.

What We Actually Do

Momentum is not a marketing agency. We're not consultants, either. We're something in-between—and much more valuable.

We act as your outsourced **Commercial Director** and **Sales & Marketing Team**, all in one.

Here's how it looks in practice:

1. Sales Systems & Support

- Building your sales process from lead to close
- Setting up CRMs and tracking pipelines
- Writing scripts, email sequences, and follow-up flows
- Coaching founders or sales teams in real-world sales language

2. Marketing Strategy That Converts

- Creating campaigns tied to actual commercial goals (not just likes or clicks)
- Managing LinkedIn presence and lead generation
- Designing and delivering full-funnel outreach strategies
- Building authority content based on your lived expertise

3. Founder Visibility & Authority

- Helping founders become the face of their business online and in person
- Developing personal brand strategies that convert awareness into sales
- Writing, producing, and distributing thought leadership content across key channels

4. Aligned Execution

- Implementing sales and marketing that talk to each other
- Structuring activity around shared metrics and mutual feedback
- Getting things done week by week—not waiting for perfect

This is how alignment becomes reality. We guide, we build, and we stay accountable.

Supporting and Elevating Internal Teams

A lot of our clients already have people in place. A marketing exec. A sales manager. A small team doing the best they can with what they've got.

We don't replace them. We **support them, lead them, and build the bridge** between them.

Momentum often acts as the missing commercial layer—a strategic partner who can bring sales and marketing into one rhythm, with one message and one plan. We work with internal teams to:

- Clarify commercial goals and priorities
- Build structured campaigns that align with sales targets

- Introduce systems that simplify reporting, review, and accountability

- Provide leadership that pulls everyone forward together

Whether you're understaffed, overwhelmed, or just underperforming—we're here to lift what you've already got. We've seen the pressure that internal teams face. The blurred lines. The lack of direction. The constant "more, now, faster" without a clear commercial map.

We give those teams structure, clarity, and strategy. We create direction. And then we deliver together.

Who We Work With

We're not for everyone. And we're proud of that.

Momentum works best with businesses that:

- Are **owner-led** or founder-driven

- Have **existing traction**, but need clearer structure and more growth

- Want **long-term alignment**, not just short-term results

- Are tired of throwing money at marketing that doesn't support sales

If you've got a small team, a solid offer, and a big ambition—but feel stuck in the fog—we can help.

We've worked with estate agents, tech platforms, golf brands, property firms, trades specialists, event organisers, and growing service businesses. We understand how different industries operate, but we also know that the principles of aligned growth never change.

How It Works

We start with a conversation—not a quote.

Once we understand where you are and what you need, we recommend one of three engagement models:

A) Fractional Commercial Director

You get senior leadership in your business—without paying a full-time salary. We act as your growth lead, working with your existing team or building around you.

B) Outsourced Sales & Marketing Team

You hand over the marketing and sales execution to us. We work closely with you, but we drive the plan. Campaigns, messaging, tracking, CRM, follow-up—it's all done with commercial intent.

C) Founder Support & Visibility Accelerator

For founders who want to lead from the front but need help showing up. We work on your content, messaging, brand presence, and sales confidence.

We customise the structure to fit your business—not the other way around.

Our Difference

We've done the job. We've owned the businesses. We've stood where you stand.

I'm not a theorist. I've run pubs, estate agencies, and marketing teams. I've made payroll from scratch and lost sleep over invoices. Everything we do is built from lived experience—not trend chasing.

The Momentum team is small, focused, and commercially driven. We're not trying to win awards. We're trying to win market share—for you.

We use the principles in this book every day. We've applied them across different sectors. And we know they work—because our clients stick around, and they grow.

Where We Work

We're based in Wrexham, but we work with clients across the UK. Our model is agile, remote-ready, and built for efficiency.

We don't waste time. We get to the heart of what's missing—and we fix it.

Why You Might Call Us

- You're tired of doing everything yourself.
- You want structure, clarity, and real commercial focus.
- You've got a team, but no traction.
- You've had campaigns, but no consistency.
- You want your brand—and your sales—to finally reflect your value.

We won't send you a proposal unless we believe we can help. We don't say yes to every opportunity. We say yes when the fit is right and the opportunity is real.

Want to Talk?

If the ideas in this book resonate with where you are and where you want to go, let's have a conversation.

There's no pitch. No pressure. Just a straight, strategic chat about what's working, what's not, and what we could do together to change that.

www.gainmomentum.co.uk   hello@gainmomentum.co.uk

Connect on LinkedIn: Gavin Belton-Rose

The glue is real. So is the growth.

If you want a team that works as hard on your business as you do, Momentum is built for that. Let's build something aligned.

Final Thought: The Glue That Holds It All Together

This book has been about truth. Not trends. Not theory. Not motivational fluff or borrowed wisdom. Real-world truth. The kind you only learn by showing up every day, leading from the front, making mistakes, and learning by doing. The kind of truth that doesn't show up in Instagram quotes or LinkedIn platitudes—but does show up in balance sheets, staff retention, repeat customers, and long-term growth.

It's the truth I've earned over 25 years of being in the trenches—owning businesses, leading teams, and helping others do the same. I haven't just studied sales and marketing alignment. I've lived it.

I've learned the hard way what happens when it doesn't exist—and I've seen the transformational impact when it does.

And if there's one thing I want you to take away from this book, it's this:

Sales and marketing are not separate. They are not different departments, competing priorities, or conflicting strategies.

They are the glue.

The alignment between the two is what separates companies that grow from companies that grind.

If you've ever felt like you were spending money on marketing but not seeing results, this book has shown you why. If you've ever wondered why your sales team is busy but not closing, this book has shown you where the gaps are. If you've ever sat at your desk thinking, "I know we're capable of more, but I don't know how to get there," this book has shown you a roadmap.

Now the question becomes: what will you do with it?

Where You Go From Here

Let's get one thing straight. Reading this book isn't the work. It's the warm-up.

The real work starts now. The moment you finish this sentence and step back into your business.

There are no shortcuts. Alignment is not a one-time fix. It's a cultural shift. A way of operating. A standard that you uphold every single day.

It means leading from the front. It means getting visible—internally and externally. It means having difficult conversations when departments aren't pulling together. It means holding your agency or your internal team accountable to outcomes—not outputs.

And most of all, it means showing up as the person who sets the direction and pace. You, as the founder, the business owner, the managing director—**you are the glue** too.

Real Alignment Looks Like This

- It looks like a sales team that understands the marketing message—and a marketing team that sits in on sales calls.
- It looks like campaigns that start with commercial outcomes, not creative ideas.
- It looks like consistent language across touchpoints—from your ads to your decks to your discovery calls.
- It looks like quick wins tracked weekly and long-term strategy reviewed monthly.
- It looks like one calendar, one rhythm, one culture of accountability.

And it feels like flow.

When you get it right, your team moves faster. Communication gets clearer. Conversions go up. And the friction—the wasted time, money, and energy—starts to melt away.

You'll feel it before you see it on the spreadsheet. But trust me, it shows up there too.

A Personal Word to the Business Owners Reading This

I wrote this book for you.

Not the marketing managers. Not the sales consultants. Not the brand strategists or tech founders with VC-backed budgets.

For you. The operator. The business builder. The person who wears 17 hats and still remembers the name of every client.

You don't need another theory. You need clarity. Direction. Leadership. And the confidence to trust your instincts while building a structure that works.

If this book has helped you move even 10% closer to that, then it's done its job.

But don't stop here.

You know what you need to do. You've read the chapters. You've seen the frameworks.

Now go do the work.

What I Know For Sure

After decades in business, here's what I've come to believe:

- Growth is not random. It's engineered.
- Marketing is not magic. It's messaging, multiplied by momentum.
- Sales is not about persuasion. It's about precision, process, and people.
- Your job is not to do it all—it's to build the system that makes it all work together.

If you're still in the game, you've already got what it takes.

This book isn't a map. It's a mirror.

It reflects back the work you know you need to do—and gives you a structure to do it with focus.

If You Want a Shortcut, Here It Is:

- **Be visible.** Online and offline.
- **Be consistent.** In message, brand, effort, and review.
- **Be commercially driven.** Every marketing activity should be tied to a business outcome.
- **Be human.** Relationships still win. Offline matters.
- **Be decisive.** Perfection is the enemy of momentum.

If you remember nothing else from this book, remember that list.

Stick it on your wall. Put it in your team handbook. Build your next quarter around it.

That's what real alignment looks like in action.

Final Challenge

You've got six months in front of you. The roadmap is in your hands. Don't wait.

Pick up the phone. Send the email. Build the system.

Walk into that Monday morning meeting with a plan that aligns sales and marketing—and leads your business forward.

The glue isn't something you buy. It's something you build.

And you've just built the blueprint.

I'll leave you with this:

You don't need more time. You need more traction.

And that comes from doing fewer things, better—and doing them together.

Let's make it stick.

- Gavin Belton-Rose

Acknowledgements

Writing this book has been a labour of clarity, not creativity. I didn't set out to become an author—I set out to put into words what I've lived, led, and learned through over two decades in sales, marketing, and business ownership.

I want to start by thanking my family—who have lived through the highs, lows, pivots, and relentless hours of building multiple businesses. Your patience, love, and belief are the foundation of everything I do.

To the Momentum team—thank you for being more than colleagues. You've turned a philosophy into practice. Every client we support, every strategy we implement, every message we share—it all happens because of your focus, care, and commitment. I wouldn't write this book without knowing I have a team behind me that lives what it teaches.

To the clients who've trusted us—thank you for the opportunity to work alongside you. You've taught me as much as I've taught you. Your challenges, your wins, and your willingness to do the work have sharpened everything you've read in these pages.

To the business owners and founders who show up every day with grit and ambition—this book is for you. I've sat where you sit. I've had the same questions. And I've found that the answers usually come not from complexity, but from clarity and alignment.

To Andrew Charlton and the Hashtag Events community—thank you for giving me the platform to connect with thousands of businesses in real life. Face-to-face conversations have shaped this book more than any algorithm or trend ever could.

To Steven J Innes—your energy, style, and genuine love of people remind us all that visibility isn't about ego—it's about connection. Thank you for setting the bar high.

To Chris Jones—a true mate and a fellow Wrexham AFC fan. Your book, *Scale Blueprint*, inspired me to finally write this one. I'm grateful for your encouragement, your example, and your belief that the best stories come from the people who've actually done the work.

To every person who's read this book cover to cover—thank you. I don't take your time or attention lightly. I wrote this for people who want real results. I hope that's what it's given you.

And finally, to the businesses who haven't yet found their glue—I hope this book helps you build it.

- Gavin Belton-Rose

Printed in Dunstable, United Kingdom